TRUE TALES
OF AMERICAN
VIOLENCE

Joe,
Over 6
decades of
freindship —
Sister Alma
would be proud,
Jack

TRUE TALES
A_{OF}MERICAN
VIOLENCE

CHRIS PFOUTS
PALADIN PRESS
BOULDER, COLORADO

To Tim Willmorth
(1950-1986)

Also by Chris Pfouts:

Lead Poisoning: 25 True Stories from the Wrong End of a Gun

True Tales of American Violence
by Chris Pfouts

Copyright © 1993 by John Christopher Pfouts

ISBN 0-87364-742-4
Printed in the United States of America

Published by Paladin Press, a division of
Paladin Enterprises, Inc., P.O. Box 1307,
Boulder, Colorado 80306, USA.
(303) 443-7250

Direct inquiries and/or orders to the above address.

Contents

Acknowledgments

ALL THESE PEOPLE HELPED WITH PUTTING THIS BOOK together, and it could not have been done without them. They are: Kim Green, Big Ching, Nick Lindsay, Roger Bloomfield, Travis Beck, Janice Marie Johnson, Butch Garcia, S. Clay Wilson, Debbie Ullman, Derek Wilcox, Joyce Stephens, Eight Shot, Mike Hendrix, Gail E. Hudson, Harriet Savedra, Marc "Animal" MacYoung, Tom Miller, Alex, Joe Ranker, Tattoo Janet and CFL, Brett Botula, P.J. Reshen, Robin Mahaffey, Kelton McMullen, and my editor, Jon Ford.

Introduction

AFTER BEING SHOT IN A STREET INCIDENT IN 1988, I put together a collection of stories from gunshot survivors called *Lead Poisoning: 25 True Stories from the Wrong End of a Gun* (Paladin Press, 1991).

Since that time I've done a great deal of research into the nature and effect of gunshot wounds on people. The scariest single bit of information on the subject comes from *Unnatural Death: Confessions of a Medical Examiner* by Michael Baden, M.D. Baden has performed thousands of autopsies and is a former chief medical examiner of New York City. He wrote, "Those of our clientele who die of gunshot wounds frequently have old bullets inside them, from previous adventures."

I take this to mean that bullets are not the seeds from which wisdom springs. We who have been shot don't necessarily learn to avoid repeating the experience, with worse results the second time around. It's a sadly human situation and a really bone-ass stupid one. I also take it to mean that once you have been shot you become a member of a new high-risk group for further lead poisoning.

Shootings are only one extreme brand of violence. I don't want to be part of Baden's frequent target club, so I consider myself at risk and try to remain alert and somewhat prepared for whatever danger might come along. It can be anything, anywhere. People who don't know much about the streets look at me—6 foot 2, 220 pounds, tattoos—and say things like, "Who would mess with you?" The answer is anybody with the right mind-set, under the right circumstances, and usually with a weapon. I haven't had anyone throw a serious punch at me in years, like 13 years. Maybe it's because I'm big, but more likely it's because people around where I live don't use their hands much. They use weapons: knives and guns and baseball bats. It doesn't even have to have anything to do with you. You're there, you're as innocent as modern society allows, and you are minding your own business. Inside of a second there are bullets perforating the air we breathe, and now their business is your business. Your business is to stay alive, and you'd better mind it well.

This happened to me about two years ago in a town called—well, we could call it Shitville, except most of the residents wouldn't be able to spell the shit part. It's a small city in a profoundly retarded part of America, and there's nothing to do there except go to the gym and drink. It was a weekday, right at 5:00 P.M., and I pulled in to the beer store parking lot. The lot was crowded with cars and trucks—plumbers' vans, a glass truck, like that. It looked like a beer store parking lot should look at quitting time in a dying town. Busy.

I carried a case of returnable empties toward the front door and saw two guys hustling across the lot. I figured they'd got to the register and left their cash in the car. It happens. There was no sense or feeling of impending violence at all—the guys were in a hurry, and I noticed that, but not like they were on the way to kick ass. I got four steps inside the store and there were five gunshots and a car crash in the parking lot. That fast. And then a bunch of yelling.

Part of the yelling was me, while hotfooting toward the

back of the store, informing the other customers, "They're fucking shooting out there," real loud. One of the customers followed me back to crouch down behind a mountainous display of Coke cans. At that time there was no way of knowing if this was a robbery, an attempted robbery, a murder, or just exactly what was going on. Outside, people were still yelling, like they do after shootings.

It turned out that my radar was badly broken, my preparedness at an all-time low. All the guys in the parking lot except two were cops. One of the guys who wasn't a cop was me. The other was a small-time coke dealer who tried to drive away from the bust and got shot for his trouble. He was lying face down in the lot, handcuffed, bleeding, and crying when I came out. My being in or out of the line of fire was a matter of no more than 30 seconds.

The lesson here is that you don't even have to be involved directly in a dispute to end up as a victim. The term innocent bystander means, more often than not, somebody who didn't have the good sense to jump behind a stack of Coke cans when the shooting started: shuckin' and jivin' when you should be duckin' and divin', is how my friend Crazy Ace puts it.

Then there is the random idiot factor, a phenomenon that is becoming more common in America every day. Think back to the Fourth of July, 1992, about 11 P.M., after the fireworks. You probably remember where you were and who you were with. I sure do: I was riding the A train southbound under Washington Heights. For you lucky readers who don't visit or live in New York City, this is one of the Rotten Apple's infamous subways passing beneath a neighborhood that's well known for wholesale and retail drug vending. I had just dropped my motorcycle off across the Hudson River in the state of New Jersey. My bike is an extremely loud, very obvious, vintage chopper that only loosely conforms to the motor vehicle equipment laws. The Fourth is a night when the bulls are out on the roads big time, and the chances of my being pulled over were very good. They're good any time, but better on the Fourth. For that reason, and because I was crossing a state line, I had no concealed weapons and was alarmingly sober.

So at 11 o'clock I was on a downtown train, reading a paperback book. The only other two people in the car were at the other end, about 50 feet away, talking to each other.

At 168th Street, under Columbia Presbyterian Hospital, my man got aboard. He took a seat directly across from me, and as soon as the doors closed and we started to roll, he produced a paper of white powder—either coke or crank, probably coke—and sniffed it *alllllll* up. Then he licked the paper clean, rolled it into a ball, and flicked it down the empty aisle of the train car.

Not every town in America has people openly horning coke in public, and truth be told it's not that common in New York, if for no other reason than other folks will want a taste—or take a taste away by force. The various narcotics outlets in New York cater to a large and impatient clientele. But it's not shockingly uncommon, either. You do see people shooting up and that sort of thing, and smoking reefer is about as common, and as *de facto* legal, as smoking cigarettes.

So his sniffing didn't bother me. It was the Fourth of July, right? Let freedom ring. But I kept half an eye on him while I read my book. Abruptly he got my full attention: he reached behind himself and pulled a nice long knife from the back of his pants with his right hand and *stuck his left thumb in his mouth like a baby.* I don't know which move looked crazier, the blade or the thumb-sucking. And then there were his eyes, which were obviously headed into orbit from the coke.

Freedom was suddenly not ringing as loudly as it had been. Thumb-sucker looked at me, turning his blade this way and that to make the light gleam off the flat side, like the psycho killers do in grade-B horror flicks. The knife was hidden from the other people at the far end of the car by the design of the seats—not that they would have done anything. I learned from getting shot in the streets of New York that most people won't even dial 911 to help you out. You're strictly on your own, lonelier than a dope dealer in a parking lot full of cops. I shifted my weight in the seat to prepare a kick and closed the book, ready to throw it spine-first into his face while I got clear.

He glanced down at the knife in his hand. "You like it?" he asked.

"Yeah. I got one a lot like it." No need to tell him it was at home. It really wasn't all that difficult for me to stay calm and just act irritated. I was in kind of a general rage anyway, pissed off at being on the train instead of my bike, pissed off at New York, pissed off at being sober this close to midnight on the Fourth. They say that fights are won in the mind and not the hands anyway, and if that were true, I had this sky-high thumb-sucker already cracked in half. It was the perfect mood to be in. Once before I'd come out of a bar in that mood, just a red general urge to smash things, not well controlled, and a guy stepped around the corner and said, "Hey, you looking for trouble?" I dropped him so fast he didn't have time to bleed. But this was a blade, not an unarmed loudmouth.

Thumb-sucker looked at the knife in his hand again. "You want it?" he asked.

Little trick question there, I guessed. He probably meant pointy end first. Something else occurred to me about this guy: he was speaking clearly with his thumb in his mouth. After you get past the age of pacifiers, this is real tough to do. Stick your thumb in your mouth and try talking. This guy spent a lot of time with his thumb in his mouth. Which just made a bad scene worse.

Now I looked him in those cokey eyes. "Naw, you keep it," I said, referring to the blade. "It's a nice one, hold onto it."

"What's your tattoo say?" he asked. So he was illiterate too. "Psychotic Reaction," I said. I got it after I got shot. It made a lot of sense then. But I took the cue and started riffing, "Yeah," I lied, "it was this band I used to be in, maybe you heard of us? Anyway, we played around a lot. I played bass, and we were doing pretty good, making some money, you know, and then my drummer married this broad, I never could stand this bitch, you know? You ever have a friend of yours marry some broad you couldn't stand? She was nothing but trouble, this dame, telling him what to do all the friggin' time, and finally he quit the band and I lost my job and had to sell my bass, and I haven't worked in six fucking months . . ." Just a torrent of bullshit talk, and this guy's eyes were rolling. Anybody's would have been. We pulled into the 125th Street station and I got up nice and casual, stuffed my book into my hip pocket, and said goodbye on the way out. Then I moved back one car and resumed my ride.

I have absolutely no doubt that the thumb-sucker cut the hell out of someone that night—someone who quivered and sniffled and begged him not to do it. That's what he was looking for, fear and the power that goes with it. You can get all cerebral about it if you like, talking about illiteracy and the permanent underclass of society and all that, but its relevance evaporates the second the cat pulls his shank. Right out the fucking window.

What saved me that night was attitude. If he had caught me in a more vulnerable mood, it might have turned out differently. If I had hit one more red light on the way to the beer store that other day in Shitville, I might have been standing between the long arm of the law—with a gun at the end of it—and a fleeing perp. The point is that violence can find you in the streets of modern America anywhere, anytime, wandering in for beer in mid-America or riding the subways of New York City.

In the pages of this book are first-person accounts of

American violence, from both the giving and receiving ends. People in here have been shot, stabbed, beaten, even attacked with a running Skilsaw. Others have shot people, stabbed them, beaten them. Give and take.

Violence is a complex occurrence. If you don't already know it, the very first thing you have to do is forget what you see in the movies and pay attention to the real deal.

Television and movies are probably the biggest enemies of reality there is, especially when it comes to violence. One-punch knockouts, high-kicking karate moves, the stabbing victim who slumps down immediately dead, shooting victims who obediently snuff out and stay out— all are Hollywood fictions.

Take the one-punch Hollywood knockout. The injured party lies on the floor, just as if he were asleep, and everyone goes about their business. I saw a one-punch fight a while back. A drunk redneck kept mouthing off to a young kid in a bar. Everybody told the 'neck to shut up, and the kid did his best to ignore him. Finally the kid's patience wore through and he belted the 'neck in the jaw with a looping roundhouse right. He had to reach up to deliver it.

The 'neck went down like a sack of wet shit. Both the kid and the 'neck had friends, and a number of pool cues were broken in half, although none were swung. The barmaid called the cops, the kid left, and a few minutes later the 'neck got to his feet, bled all over the pool table, the bar, and several of the customers, and reeled out into the night, screaming that he was going to kill the little prick who done him wrong, leaving a trail of fresh blood behind him.

That's what a real one-punch fight is like. Cops, blood, friends involved, a general mess. It's nothing like the movies. And that's just one hard right hand. When you bring weapons into it, everything goes up exponentially. More blood, more cops, more trouble.

Another thing television and film teaches people is that appearances matter: the badder you look, the badder you are. Let me tell you, appearances don't mean shit. Less than six months ago I saw a yuppie in a Brooks Brothers suit beating the crap out of a Manhattan bar bouncer in the street. When the second bouncer flew out the door and tried to clothesline the yuppie, literally in a Superman horizontal dive, the yuppie slipped the grab and kept fighting. And the two bouncers never did knock him off his feet; he just left. To look at this yuppie, you would have thought he was an easy mark.

Another recent incident: a winter day, not too cold, and a pretty young woman sitting on a front stoop minding her own business. Here came a street bum, with the stocky, strong build and shaved head of actor Charles Dutton. He was filthy dirty, and one of his eyes had been gouged out some time in the past. He asked the woman for some money and, when she said no, demanded some. He got unruly, and when she retreated into the building vestibule, he followed her. Now she was trapped. She didn't have a key to get through the inside door, and because the outer doors were mostly iron, no one could tell what was happening inside. I'd seen the whole thing, and pulled the flat leather-covered police sap I usually carry. I didn't climb the steps or approach the man, just yelled at him: "Hey, leave her alone. What the fuck's wrong with you?"

That was all it took, just somebody to say something. He didn't even look to see who was doing the talking, just turned away from the woman and came outside. This dude, unlike the battling yuppie, looked scary as hell, especially with that one blank eye. But he wasn't up for a fight. Intimidating a small, scared woman, yes. A fight, no. A smart move on his part, because I'd have gone straight for his remaining eye and tried to leave him blind—it's his most vulnerable spot, and not too damn hard to reach, either. The woman in this case, I'm certain, didn't understand what it was I had in my hand.

I don't know what they teach in dojos these days. My

only formal self-defense instruction came from a wiry old coot named Charlie Nelson here in New York. Charlie taught sensible moves, but he also would say things like, "If that don't work, spit in his eye, kick him in the shins, and throw his ass out into traffic." If you're dojo-trained, picture yourself where I was that Fourth of July: in a sitting position, no weapon, facing a jacked-up psycho who's holding a big shiny knife and sucking his thumb. What's your training tell you?

That's the value of this book—real-life violence from both sides, nothing preplanned, no by-the-rules moves. It ain't like the movies, which is precisely the point. Reading about how others survived attacks can help if your turn comes around. And reading about the other side, the dealing side, can help you understand what's coming at you. It's information I hope you never need. But if you do, I sure hope it helps.

Jack Quigley

Me ↗

IT'S GOT TO BE ALMOST 20 YEARS AGO. I WAS WORKING
undercover, and an informant introduced me to a guy who
allegedly had a bunch of guns and some stolen property for
sale. So my partner and I went down to see this guy later
on, where he hung out, at a bar, a real sleazy bar in a not-
so-affluent section of town. This happened in Palisades
Park [New Jersey].

That afternoon when I was down there with the informant, the guy had a gun and he was in the bar shooting the
gun out the back window. There was a little kid playing in
the parking lot, but that didn't seem to faze him—so I got
an idea of his mentality and what he was capable of doing.
The bar was famous for fights and stabbings, all kinds of
brutality, moving stolen property and drugs, that sort of
thing. He was shooting out the back window, so obviously
he wasn't too well balanced and he liked to shoot his gun.
So I was extra cautious.

I went there that evening with another undercover officer to talk to him about buying some guns and stolen property, whatever he was capable of doing. He was always
bragging, I found out later, that he could deliver stolen
goods. And also, subsequent to this evening, I found out
that he had received some stolen property from some mob

11

figures—or alleged mob figures, hangers-on, peripheral people—and had not paid for it, had sold it and kept the money. So there was a rumor that there was a hit out on him. We didn't know this at the time.

So we went back to the bar and started talking to the guy. I introduced him to my partner and I asked him to step over by the jukebox where we could talk. And he said sure. We started to discuss what he had for sale, and he patted me on the back. I had a .45 tucked in my waistband in the back and I think he felt it. Apparently he did.

He said, "Let's go out by my car, we have to talk by my car." I figured something was wrong, I just got a bad feeling. After a few years of police work you just have a sixth sense—it's not something you could put your thumb on, but you get a feeling something's wrong. I couldn't possibly articulate it at the time.

I walked toward the door with him and I said to my partner, "I think he knows I'm carrying. Watch my back." Or words to that effect. So we went out to the car, it was an old Cadillac, a '60s Cadillac. Without saying a word he got into the car—he sat inside the car, the door was open, and I was standing by the edge of the open door—he turns around and pulls the armrest down with his left hand, reaches in, and pulls out a .32 auto. He points it toward my head, says, "I don't fuck around," and pulls the trigger.

Which can kind of ruin your day for you. Fortunately, he didn't spend much time at the range. Because what I think happened, he tried to shoot me and my partner and rushed the first shot, thinking he got me. When I saw him coming out with his piece I went for mine, and the shots went off one after the other.

His shot went off next to my head and went right by the side of my face. All I saw was the muzzle blast. The last conscious thought I had was that I was going to die. I still get emotional about it 20 years later. But I remember thinking, if I'm going to die I'm taking you with me, motherfucker. All I remember in that split second was having such total contempt for this guy who had the audacity to try and kill me. And I started firing my gun. I was consciously aware of three rounds, then I thought the gun jammed. When I looked down the slide was back and it was empty, and I realized I'd shot eight rounds. Then I looked back up at him and he was sprawled out of the car.

During the gunfire my partner got a round off also. He didn't see the guy come out with the gun initially, but he saw me go for mine and he went for his. Then when he saw what was happening, by the time I had fired eight, he got one off and hit the guy. The guy just sprawled out of the car onto the pavement and didn't move any further. We found out later that while we were shooting, his reflexes caused him to jerk and he shot himself in the foot during all this exchange of gunfire. If a tragedy can be comical, it was a little bit comical that he thought he was going to kill us and wound up shooting himself in the foot.

Immediately after that a uniformed officer on patrol heard the shots and he comes running with his gun out pointing at us, my partner and me. First he points at my partner and my partner says, "Don't shoot, we're police officers." Then he points at me and I said, "I am too."

He says, "What about him?" and points at the guy on the ground. I said, "No, he's the bad guy." He said, "Oh, good."

I reloaded. I didn't know if he was dead or not, or what kind of shape he was in. I held my gun on the guy until we determined that. I didn't even see where his gun went. When he rolled out of the car it fell on the floor of the car, and there was just blood all over the place. My partner's round went through his back and severed the aorta. When I shot him he went forward and my partner dumped one in his back. I remember seeing blood spurt out of his back, just pump out, during this blurred remembrance that I have. Then the guy rolled out of the car. That was it.

[Jack had to go in front of a grand jury later and remembers this aspect of the incident as sharply as the shooting itself.] I was being a little caustic because I resented having to go in front of a group of citizens who spend their lives in front of a television set and have no concept of what reality is. We're out there every day and every night protecting these people, and they're so naive, they have no concept of what goes down in the streets. I was getting some really silly questions: "Why didn't you shoot the gun out of his hand?" Inane, stupid questions. And when this lady asked me, "Why did you shoot him eight times?" I just said, "It was all the rounds I had." The grand jury recommended psychiatric treatment for me; they recommended it to my chief, and he just totally disregarded it. He said, "When they get involved in shootings, then they'll be able to criticize you."

Funny, I was married at the time to a former wife, and I called her and told her I was involved in a shooting and I had killed the guy. This gave me a clue that the marriage was on the rocks. The first thing she wanted to know was, "Is anybody coming after me? Do they know where I live and are they coming to get me?" I said, "I'm fine." That gave me a little clue that perhaps I shouldn't stay married to this woman for the rest of my life. The woman I'm married to now married me when I was a police officer, so she knows exactly what the game is. She's really good. I roll in with one of these motorcycle projects and she doesn't say a word. If she says, "Where's the money coming from for this one?" I just say I'm gonna work a lot of overtime in the next couple months.

For about a year after [the shooting], I was getting tension headaches. You have to go through all these inquisitions from idiots. First, you get the type of police officer who thinks it's glamorous to have killed somebody. These people are assholes. "Gee it must be exciting, it must really be something . . ." You just walk away from idiots like that. Because it's not exciting. It's nice to be alive, and you're very grateful that you succeeded in defending your life. But it certainly is not a pleasure, and it's no thrill to look a guy in the eye and pull the trigger. Not at all. I mean, it's a thrill to be alive and telling you about this, but the act itself, there's no glamour involved. It's instincts and survival. It's that simple. You want to live. And if your will to live is strong enough, you will. [These are] the guys with pearl handles, the nickel-plated guns, gunslinger rigs. They're morons. The biggest supporters of war and about what they would do if they were shipped there are guys that have never gone, will never go, and are psychologically or physically unable to perform the necessary duties. These are the guys who are toughest with their mouths.

But this particular shooting incident was a little different from war. I was in Vietnam. And that's a very impersonal thing when you're shooting. Very impersonal. You've already made your enemy subhuman through your attitudes and the attitudes of your instructors in boot camp, infantry training, all of that. You've reduced your enemy to a subhuman level, which makes it much easier to kill him. I don't even know if I killed anybody over there. We'd take sporadic gunfire from hills or trees or shrubs or paddies or whatever, and just open up with thousands of rounds going back in the other direction. I'd never gone one-to-one and pulled the trigger on somebody before. It's a totally different situation. It's very personal when you look a guy in the eye and take care of business. It's something. As I said, it's 20 years ago, and it seems like last night. Every once in a while I'll think about it and get upset but be thankful that I'm alive.

Sometimes it's easy to talk about and sometimes it's not. I started to say that for a year after that I was getting tension headaches. I was on medication, I was drinking, I was on Tylenol with codeine and chasing it with beers and shots of Jack Daniel's. I started to realize that this was a dead-end street. I was becoming a drug addict and an alcoholic. Why? Because some asshole tried to kill you and you lived? I stopped, stopped taking medication—it was prescription drugs, and I think the doctor knew I was taking too many, but he knew the situation so he gave them to me. Stopped drinking. And I was fine after a few months, bailed out.

I laugh at these Rambo types. Everybody's a tough guy until it comes down to planting your feet on the ground and saying, "Okay, pal, let's go. You and me." It separates the men from the boys. When it comes time to put your uniform on and pick up the rifle, then it's *hominahominahomina*. "I really didn't mean it, I was just supporting everybody else."

My partner—not my partner that night, but when I was in uniform—was involved in a shooting about 10 days prior to that. A totally different incident. He was in uniform and responded to a report of a man with a gun, shots fired. He and his partner at the time ran around the house. The wife of the shooter is at the front door screaming, "He's in the back, he's got a gun and he's shooting!"

They come around back and they converge on the corner of the back of the house, and the guy comes right around the corner. [My partner] put I think three rounds in the guy. The guy dropped and died. The wife sued him. Saved her life and she sued him. Incredible.

You'll find that guys who have pulled the trigger on people will very rarely talk about it. They're very quiet about it. And if they are bragging about it, they're insane and they shouldn't be carrying a gun. It's that simple. I'd say 90 percent of the guys that work for me now don't even know I was involved in a shooting. It's none of their business.

Going back to the Rambo type [of police officer] who thinks it's wonderful and exciting and wants to hear about it; the other half avoid you, don't talk to you at all. For what reason, I don't know. It's like they're afraid to talk to you. Maybe they're afraid it's going to upset you, or maybe they're just afraid to talk about it. Maybe they think you're insane now and you're unbalanced, who knows? But those are the percentages. Half the guys you know or are associated with think it's exciting and want to hear about it, and the other half don't even talk to you at all. Or just barely communicate with you.

My partner and I were very close before the shootings—he's a Vietnam vet also—and we just kind of hooked up and became even closer after the shootings. We commiserated with one another. We both stopped drinking, because he was going through the same thing. There was no help available, nobody to talk to, no counseling, no peer groups, nothing at all. So you seek somebody out that had a similar experience and you vent with him and he vents with you. And you survive. Maybe.

The guy he was with, his partner that night, committed suicide a few years later. He had fired also. I don't know why he killed himself; it could have been that he could have been despondent, or maybe he had some other personal problems to compound it and he just couldn't live with it. But he took his own life with a gun. Cops have a tendency to do that; it's called eating your gun. Stick it in your mouth and pull the trigger.

The way my life is now, and I can't foresee it changing, I'm having a fantastic time. I just can't imagine anyone wanting to take their own life for any reason whatsoever. As bad as things could get, there's always tomorrow. You wake up, give it another shot. But I guess I've never been in a situation where I was browbeaten and downbeaten. I love every single day. I guess that's part of having been through a war, maybe because of the shooting. You appreciate being alive so much that you don't let any shit bother you at all, nothing. You laugh at things other people are just tormented by, but hey, fuck it. You can't send me back to Vietnam. What are you gonna do? What could *possibly* happen? So I go bankrupt, is that the worst thing? So I'll get a job, refinance everything, so what? I'll have credit back in three years and I'll be fine. You lose a loved one, that happens. You survive. Find a new loved one if you can.

Jack Quigley is a lieutenant with the Bergen County, New Jersey, Prosecutor's Office.

Steve Bonge

I GUESS YOU COULD SAY IT STARTED OVER A PARKING
situation. Somebody pulled a van in, a crew of construc-
tion workers. They pulled their van into the spot, and I said
I had to put a vehicle there and I was waiting for that spot.
They just pulled in front of me like it was nothing and
parked their van there. So I went over to the guy and I said,
"Hey, you're not supposed to put a vehicle there," and he
said, "Fuck you, I don't care about you or your fuckin'
parking spot."

I said, "Hey, man, you got two fuckin' minutes to move
the van or I'm gonna stab all your tires." I had a knife there
and he saw it, so he knew I meant it. But I got the same
fucking thing. He goes, "Fuck you and your spot." And
they all went inside and went back to work, into this apartment building. They were putting a whole brick front on
the building, so there was a bricklayer out there working.
They were inside, putting in fire doors, like halfway down
the hall. There's a regular steel frame door on the building,
and halfway down the hall they were putting in steel frame
doors. There was a room to the right, so I guess they were
putting one on an apartment in there that they were reno-
vating, all gutted out.

Anyway, I was all hot and fired up about this guy taking

my spot and saying I don't give a fuck about you and this and that. There was a whole bunch of them and they went inside and they were laughing about it like it was a big joke. And there's one of me, so I knew there was going to be a confrontation. I hung out a minute or two and tried to cool off about it, but that didn't work, so I went across the street and grabbed the nearest thing I saw, which was a thick, big, fucking long stick. Shorter than a baseball bat, but it was like a long, round, hardwood stick.

So one of my friends that lives in the building here said, "Hey, what's going on?" I said, "These motherfuckers disrespected me, they won't move their van. They knew I was waiting for that spot and they just pulled in anyway."

He said, "Fuck these assholes. Let's go over there and straighten it out." Went over there, the bricklayer was just doing work putting bricks on the front of the building, you know, so we went in there. They were all in there working. They had the door in the hall. It was a long, narrow hall. The door opens in. Both of us went in and started walking down the hallway.

The guy I had the words with, the fuckin' driver, he was working on a door frame with the door in it, and on the other side of the door were a couple other workers. We started walking down the hallway and I yelled, "Hey, motherfucker, you gonna move the fucking van? What the fuck?" He had a few words for me, like, "Fuck you, I ain't moving nothing."

I forgot how the situation went, but I think my friend got to him and they started going at it first. The guys on the other side of the door started wondering what was going on and they were sticking their heads around. The door thing they were working on, it's a real weird situation, kind of hard to explain. They were in the hallway working on this frame, but it wasn't set in where it had to go. They were working on the hinges or whatever, doing the small work before they set the frame in, you know?

He was on the outside of the door and they were on the other side. Him and my friend started going at it, and I went to the other guys and started blasting a couple of them. One or two of them got beaned once or twice and they just ran the other way. They really didn't want the confrontation. It was this other guy who really had the fuckin' mouth right from the start. My friend hit him a couple of times and they started going back and forth. First, the guy picked up a hammer and swung it a couple times, and my friend ran into the room on the right where they were working, the gutted apartment. We both went into the room. I had the stick and I started toward him.

The guy picked up a Skilsaw that was plugged into an extension cord and pulled the blade guard back. He fired the thing up, with the blade spinning, and started coming at me with the thing.

I had the stick, and I was swinging the stick, and I wound up back out through the doorway. As soon as I came into the doorway he was there; just picked the thing up and started coming at me. So we went back out into the hallway and he was coming at me, revving the thing up like he was gonna cut me open with the saw.

So I'm walking backward, fighting him backward with the stick, you know, beaning him upside the head, in the shoulders, and I was able to hit his hand. While all this was going on, we were face-to-face in this narrow hallway where we couldn't really turn or swing or anything. He was coming toward me with the saw, revving it up, and I was beating him with the stick, and we just kept going at it the whole length of the hall.

I remember, the thing that was going through my mind was hoping the extension cord would run out. But it didn't. I got all the way to the end of the hall and the door was closed, and it opened toward us. The street door, my back was right up to the street door. My friend, he was behind me. The two of us were cramped in this hallway, and I'm beating him this way, and my friend was behind me and there was no way to do anything. Because if he'd been behind him he would have got him.

That's what happened. My friend went out the door and my back wound up against the door. I was able to hit the hand that was holding the blade guard, so he pulled that away, and the blade guard went back and the saw was just going *click click click* because the saw wouldn't go with the blade guard forward. So I couldn't get cut open with it anymore.

We were face-to-face and I was hitting him with the stick. He started bashing me over the head with the Skilsaw. He hit me like two or three times and split the whole top of my head open, blood all over the place. I kept bashing him, beating him, and hitting him. I beat him all the way back up the hallway and into that room. He fell over backward, dropped the saw, and picked up the hammer that he originally had. Meanwhile, my friend ran in. He'd grabbed a hammer from the bricklayer who was out front doing brick work, one of those square-tip bricklayer's hammers. I forgot exactly what happened; this guy went down on the ground and the saw went bouncing out of his hand—either that or he just wasn't able to swing it back at me—but I kept steady on him, beating him with the stick, and it wound up fuckin' splitting his whole face open and fucking him up. We just split, ran out of there, and when we left the building he was all covered with blood, all fucked up.

I ran out. Another one of the people from my building came across the street and said, "Hey, what's going on?" My whole head was split open with blood all over my face, and I said, "I'm splitting because the cops are gonna be here any minute, and this guy's really fucked up." I jumped in my truck and drove to Long Island. Within five minutes there was a million cops and an ambulance there, and they carted him away to the hospital.

The other workers basically stayed out of it. He was the mouth that caused the situation, and they just seemed like they wanted to work and not be bothered. It was just the one guy with his fuckin' mouth, and he caused the shit. And got the worst of it, obviously, but he also split my head open with a fuckin' Skilsaw. It's a good thing I was able to hit his hand. I don't know if it was a fluke that I hit it or what. He was a little bigger than me, built pretty good, but that doesn't mean really anything. I fucked the guy up and sent him to the hospital. Big shit.

I just took a shower and got cleaned up, and within a few hours it stopped bleeding. It could have used stitches. It was a few good, deep gashes, and you could see it for fuckin' months. I'm sure if you look right now the scars are there. No big deal. I'm not gonna die over a few scars. I've been hit with bigger objects, you know?

I don't want to come off like a big hero for splitting this guy's head open. It's no picnic, but that's what happened.

Steve Bonge is a photographer, sculptor, and motorcycle and car builder. He is a member of the largest motorcycle club in the world. He lives in New York City.

Nevin Washington

IT WAS ABOUT TWO AND A HALF BLOCKS FROM MY house. The area is basically called Clinton Hill, it's right next to Fort Greene. It's in what's technically considered a pretty nice neighborhood. Where I am it's kind of like borderline, because you go a couple blocks and you go into Bedford-Stuyvesant. But even to me Bed-Stuy has its good and bad points. Brooklyn's like that. The neighborhood is such that you can walk down one block and it's all showcase brownstones, all white-collar professionals, and so on. Turn the corner and it could be a completely run-down block. Here and there might be a house getting fixed up. One thing I've seen over the years, there's been a lot of rehab. Over the last eight years is when the major gentrification started. It's changed a lot, especially in police presence. Before when you called the cops they said they were too busy to come. Now we have cops walking the beat.

You tend to think of it as a fairly safe neighborhood. I've walked around at all times of night. Not so much now as I did before, but in past years I have. I come home on the A train three, four in the morning. My apartment's right across the street from the subway station. Never had any problems. People said they got jumped or robbed coming out of the subway station late. As the years went by I wouldn't stay out as late, and if I did I'd come home in a cab.

This particular night, it was Monday, September 16. I left work, and I called my wife ahead of time and said I'd be getting home kind of late so don't bother cooking, I'll pick something up.

I came out of the subway about 8 o'clock. It was still fairly light. It wasn't that dark yet. On Atlantic Avenue nearby they had opened up a White Castle. It had only been opened about six months, and I thought this would be as good a time as any to try it out. I was in the mood for White Castle, like a craving.

So I walked over. It took a long time to get my food, so that killed about a half hour waiting for my order. I finally got it and I was coming back. I came up Grand Avenue, maybe three blocks from my house. It was a very dark street, more so than the other blocks, which tend to be very well lit.

I had noticed that there were guys hanging out, but they were mostly very young. I always carry a stick, and it seemed to deter most people from messing with me, especially on the subway. So I wasn't even thinking about anything happening. I had gone most of the block, I was about three quarters up, and by now it was dark. It was about 8:30.

So I was almost to Fulton and feeling very safe, like, what can happen now? Then all of a sudden I heard this voice, a young voice saying, "Give me your money." I thought, well, maybe he wasn't talking to me, maybe he was talking to someone else. So I ignored it and kept on going. Then this figure jumped in front of me and I could tell it was a young kid, maybe 14, 15, that weird age when you're not quite sure how old the kid is. He wasn't even full grown, just starting to get his height, starting to stretch. He had on a pair of shorts, T-shirt. He had no facial hair. He just looked like any other kid in the street. And then he said, "I said give me your money." He had either a .22- or a .25-caliber automatic held pointed down, with both hands, pointing to my lower region.

The first thing I thought was, is it a toy gun? Then I thought, no, the way kids are today, they all got real guns. I only had seven dollars on me, I didn't have a lot of money.

Instead of being afraid, like I always thought I would be, I got mad. I always assumed that if I got attacked it would be by an adult, a crackhead, a professional mugger. In that case, my instinct would have been to say, "Okay, man, chill out, here's the money." They're usually too desperate for anything else. But because it was a kid, I totally went the other way. I found myself swelling with anger. This kid was trying to shake me down, gun or no gun. Without even thinking—my hands were full, I had my burgers, my briefcase, and I had my stick—I went to swing at him with my stick: "Get the fuck away from me you bastard."

He jumped back, surprised I guess that I went for him. He was about four feet away. And he fired three shots. Then he turned and ran, he ran away, and I started to run after him. That's when I realized that I got hit. Just after a few steps I felt an ache in my leg. When I looked down I saw blood coming through my pants leg. I had on dark purple pants, so at first I didn't even notice, then I saw this wet stuff coming through the pants leg and I said, "Oh, shit, he got me."

The kid was already running down the street, and I was yelling at him, "I'm gonna get you you little bastard," just yelling anything I could think of. At the same time I was cursing to myself, "Goddamn it, I would get hit."

I didn't feel anything at the time. I saw the gun fire, saw the flash of the gun, and that was all. I figured that the kid was so scared that he shot blind and missed me altogether, even though I was that close.

But I pulled my pants leg up after I saw the blood coming out, and I realized there was blood on both sides of my kneecap. I thought, maybe it went through me. I rolled the pants up to my thigh, which kind of acted like a tourniquet.

By this time people had come out. I was in front of this house when I got shot. I was still yelling and cursing, and these people appeared at the window and said, "Are you okay?"

I said, "No, I got shot."

They came out and they were very nice. They helped me over to their front stoop. They went inside and came out with paper towels so I could stop the blood. The guy was looking at my leg, and he said that it went in and out, that he could see the holes.

By this time I was aching and my adrenaline was starting to calm down. I was saying to myself, "At least I'm not dead." It wasn't as bad as I thought it would be, because I really didn't feel much. I really thought I would feel a lot more pain. They went in the house and called the EMS and the police, and I gave them my phone number to call my wife, and to emphasize that I was okay even though I'd been shot.

I was surprised at how fast the EMS and the police came. I thought they'd say, "Well, it's just another shooting" and take their time. But they all came within a relatively few minutes. And not just one ambulance, but two, plus two or three police cars.

It was a woman cop that I dealt with mostly. She was asking questions like, "Do you know what he looked like?" I said that I probably couldn't identify him even if he was right in front of me again. The whole thing took like 10 seconds. There really wasn't anything I could identify him with, like a certain type of hat or clothing, because he only had on shorts and a T-shirt. He had no beard or moustache. There just wasn't much to go by, and it was too dark to really see his face because it was all shadows.

By that time they'd loaded me into the ambulance and I

said, "Could we hang around a few minutes, at least until my wife gets here? I hate to have her come and I'm not even here." They asked if I was in a lot of pain. I said, "It hurts, but it's nothing I can't deal with. If you can stay a few minutes I'd appreciate it."

She did show up, and she was more upset than I was. She was like all hysterical. I said, "It's all right, I'm okay, nothing serious seems to be the matter." Then one of the cops said, "Don't forget your burgers" because I'd left my burgers on the stoop. I'd had them with me all the time. So I'm there in the ambulance eating my burgers. I figured, I'm going to the ER I'd better eat something because I wasn't going to get anything else soon, knowing how hospitals are. My wife got in the ambulance with me and we rode to the hospital.

I went in the ER and that was the worst part. It was a horror show. I always knew that ERs could be hairy, but now I was part of it. I was never really in one before. All around me, all I could see was people suffering—elderly people with asthma attacks, one guy had cut himself on a piece of glass and his whole arm was split open, somebody else had gotten knifed, and there was another shooting. Just all this humanity suffering all around me. So they put me in this room and said, "Somebody will be with you as soon as they can." I waited and waited. By this time it's really starting to hurt, and so I asked if somebody could give me a painkiller.

This nurse came in, and she was taking the information down, they were taking my Blue Cross card and all that stuff. A couple of doctors came in and they looked at it, they dressed it, and they asked if I had any feeling in my feet, and I said yeah, and I wiggled my toes. They said it was probably a clean shot, but they wanted to take an X-ray to be sure. I had that done and it was totally clean. No bone, no artery, it just went through pure muscle.

That's when I began to hear the one sentence. The one

phrase for the next five weeks was, "You're lucky. You're really lucky. You could have been dead." I heard that one to the point where I didn't want anyone to say it anymore. The X-ray guy started it. He said, "Hey, you're a lucky guy, man, a clean shot." After that, everybody who came to see me or dealt with me said the same thing.

Some plainclothes cops came by to take a statement, and they asked again if I could identify the guy. I told them that if he was right in front of me in a group I probably couldn't identify him. And that's when I realized he shot me twice.

One bullet had missed completely. The second bullet went through my leg and the third bullet went through my wallet. I always carry my wallet in my front pocket. I still have the wallet at home. When I opened it up, the few dollars I had in there were all bullet scarred. You could see where they'd traced right along. And if I hadn't had the wallet where it was, it would probably have gone though my pelvic area. At least, that's how the cops felt about it.

I spent the night for observation. I sent my wife home. There was nothing more she could do, and she was all upset. I got released the next afternoon. I felt fine outside of it hurting, and I had my stick with me anyway so I used that to get home. The worst part was that I live in a fourth-floor walk-up and I had to hobble all the way up to my apartment.

I took some ibuprofen and went back to work that Friday. I didn't baby it, and I was getting around pretty good. Everybody wanted to see the bullet hole. And that more or less ended it, except for about a month or so later, going down the street to the store I ran into the woman that helped me that night. She said, "Well, you'd probably like to know that the kid who shot you is dead."

When the cops took my statement that night they said that the stretch of Grand Avenue between Atlantic and Fulton was a trouble spot—a lot of people had been robbed there over the months. Same thing. They'd go to the White Castle and come out, and because it was a dark area they'd get jumped. Several kids were apparently operating there. She said that he had pushed his luck too far and tried to rob an off-duty cop, who shot him. And that was it. On the one hand I felt kind of bad because he was a kid, but as time went by, I said to myself, if I'd had a gun on me I'd probably have shot him too, just for self-preservation. His age wouldn't have deterred me that much.

I had nightmares once or twice, but it really hasn't affected me in what I do. I had to confront it. I didn't want to start being afraid of everything and everybody, the way some people react.

Nevin Washington is an artist and very natty dresser. He lives in Brooklyn.

Dede Shurb

I PICKED A LOT OF FIGHTS. I WAS THE INITIATOR IN A LOT of incidents. One of my biggest fights was, it was my birthday, my nineteenth birthday party. We were having a few kegs out in someone's backyard, and all sorts of different people showed up. I hate women in general, I hate the whole facade of what women . . . very phony. I don't like women as friends, I don't like women in social situations.

So I pulled this girl out of the crowd and decided I was gonna beat her up. It ended in the middle of the street. That was a bad one, because I really beat her up, you know? It was just a real strange situation. I didn't just pull her out. She was a girl that had given a bunch of my skinhead buddies venereal disease. So it wasn't like out of the blue I went crazy and said, "This one!" I had reasons behind it.

I said, "You are the most sleazy thing I have ever met." And she said, "Oh yeah?" and she pokes me. I have that pit bull technique; I go for the throat, get them down on the ground, and fuck 'em up, you know? Real quick, simple and done with.

So I went for the throat. I got her down. Couple black eyes, blood dripping from her face and stuff. Then they pulled me off, like four guys pulled me off, and I was snorting and hollering, and she was still talking shit. They let her go and she got out to her car, and I pulled her out of her car and beat her up some more. And she was never seen again. She went home to mom and dad and never came back.

There's a lot of gang fighting in Minneapolis. There's a lot of black youth gangs like the Crips, the Vice Lords, the Disciples. Then there were two different factions of skinheads. One group was called the Baldies and the other group were the people who weren't Baldies. They would band together because they just couldn't take the Baldies and their garbage. There was a lot of fights that way. There would be warehouse parties, in old empty warehouses, 16 kegs and people from all different walks would go there. Minneapolis isn't real big, but a few different high schools and a few rumors and you'd meet all sorts of people in there.

Fights would happen. Two-by-fours, pipes, people getting stabbed. Not too many shootings. Only one real close friend of mine got shot. She wasn't even a real close friend, she was just another skinhead girl. That was an accident at her house where they were playing with a gun. They put the gun away, and her brother put the bullets back in or something. They didn't know the bullets were back in and took the gun out. She got shot in the back and paralyzed.

I was out of high school at this time. I was 18, 19. It started when I was about 16, but I wasn't in high school when I was 16 either. A lot of the gang stuff that went on, everybody's younger brothers and stuff were involved, and they were all in high school. Not a lot of girls. Especially with the black gangs, because they just didn't have any girls. They might have girlfriends or whatever, but nobody that was permanently in the gang. The skinheads are different that way, where you'd get two or three girls that were there every fight, every time something happened.

And then there were the St. Pauli skins, from St. Paul, and they were all white power and they'd come over and every Minneapolis skin would be . . . One time I remember this fight in a vacant lot. There was a building there, but they'd taken it down so there were big chunks of cement and wire. It looked like a scene from the Holocaust. And there we all are with bats and stuff, knocking each other's heads off. It was pretty funny. It was behind this old Best Buys, that company that sells electronic things. It was behind there. They had torn out the building to make a parking lot, and in the meantime we decided to fight there. All the St. Paul skins had a bunch of pickup trucks like the big bunch of rednecks that they are. They would come over and jump out and we'd go at it. But they didn't have the numbers we had. They could give us a good beating here and there, singly, on the street or something, but when it came down to it we had them overpowered.

There was a river that divided us, the Mississippi River. And there were railroad bridges that go across the river, and everyone would drink on these bridges, and occasionally you'd bump into them up there. And that was always exciting, go onto a railroad bridge and bump into some Nazi skinheads that you were going to fuck up. We'd meet headbanger rednecks up there too and get in a fight.

There were two levels: there was like a catwalk and there'd be people underneath, and you'd be on top and you'd start a fight with the guys underneath, dump beer on their heads or something. It'd start there and end up with a big bloodbath at the end of the bridge: "Aw, you dirty dogs, I'm gonna fuck you up now!" you know. I remember peeing on some guy down there one time and it ended up in a big old fight. There I am walking around, I see him through the track, I whipped it down and peed on this guy's head. That was pretty funny. He's probably still cursing me out, washing his hair every day.

One really bad thing that happened, I lived in the building on Grand Avenue, in Minneapolis. It was like a two-bedroom apartment I had in the back of the building, on ground level. I had a roommate. We had all been at this party with a bunch of friends, and I had come home early. I drank too much or something, just calling it an early night.

Somebody was driving my roommate home, and as they were coming up to the building in the front, some of my neighbors were having a fight. They got out of the car to see what was going on, see if it would be good to watch or something. One of these friends of mine, Byron, was walking up to them. "Hey guys, what's going on?" And they said, "Hey, is your name Joe?" Byron was skin bald, Bic razor style. They asked him if his name was Joe, and Byron, being an asshole, said, "Yeah."

So they got in a fight and they ended up pulling knives. Byron took out his knife and stabbed two of them, one of them in the chest. Stabbed them both pretty good. The ambulance had to come, and there was chunks of their hair on the ground out front, stuck in the snow, because it was wintertime. And blood, loads of blood. And the cops came and arrested him.

Meanwhile, my roommate got into the building no problem, and I woke up the next day and there was blood all over the house, because my roommate had been in the fight too. There was blood on all the light switches, bloody jeans on the living room floor. [Byron] ended up getting a few years, and they ended up getting away scot-free. They didn't find any weapons on them. Byron was soaked with blood and still had his knife on him. He probably could have gotten rid of it. He was a good friend of mine. I still write to him in prison.

Dede Shurb is a cheerful woman with an easy laugh. She operates her own graphics and typesetting business and publishes a quarterly newsletter.

Barton Heyman

I WAS ON THE WEST SIDE HIGHWAY IN NEW YORK, IN the far lane, going south past 125th Street on the way to the 95th Street exit to drop my girl off. This is a week ago Sunday night [eight days]. So this last Sunday we're coming back from the country again and I'm wondering: Can lightning strike again? Am I being the biggest asshole in the world? Are there going to be newspaper articles about the same schmuck got shot again in the same place? What an asshole!

We were coming back from the country, nice and quiet. Fiddling with the radio a lot, listening to some tapes and all that, and all of a sudden I thought 20,000 volts came out of the radio. My hand recoiled and I said, "Goddamn! Jesus, that's impossible; 20,000 volts can't come out of the radio. Can something have come out of the fire wall?" And then I saw the hole in my arm and at first, the horror, I thought *drive-by shooting!* Is there another one coming? I'm shot. How did they shoot me? The windshield's intact. Is there someone taking aim again? I don't know where it came from, I can't figure it out at this point.

I said, "Loie,"—Loie Glasser, my girlfriend—"Loie, don't get shocked but I've just been shot." I said, "I can move my fingers and I can move my arm up and down."

God knows how I was driving straight ahead and how I was keeping in the lane and all that sort of shit. I can move and I'm not bleeding that badly, I'm a very lucky guy. She said, "Pull over at the first turnoff and we'll find a hospital."

I said, "I'm not going to leave my car in some parking lot or in front of the emergency room because I'm not going to get shot and ripped off for my car in the same night."

She had to endure while I just kept going down the West Side Highway. I turned off on thirty something or other, and I was making all the red lights. I had to shift with the left hand, I have a stick shift. She had to wrap the wound with a sock. There wasn't that much blood, and everything was reasonably contained. I wanted to get down to the Lower East Side, to 12th and Broadway, and park the car and lock it, make sure everything's secure, and then go to St. Vincent's. Which I did. She thought I was crazy for not attending to it immediately at the nearest hospital. But I was right, really.

You get priority in the emergency room, they wheel you right in there. They take a look at you and if you're not really that bad, then you wait till the X-rays. They try to stabilize you, they take your signs and give you saline solution.

They asked me if I had any insurance and I said I did through the Screen Actor's Guild, there's some cards in my vest. He says, "No no, don't bother," or something, and wrote No Insurance. So at a certain point the doctor said he'd be back in five minutes and he disappears. Finally I had to get to vituperation. I had to get up and say, "Hey, I want somebody to pay attention. If I'm not going into the hospital I want to go home. I've been shot. I've got to get up in the morning. Come on, do something." That's when I saw the papers that said for me to come to the clinic tomorrow—I had no idea that that was because they were thinking I didn't have any insurance. I didn't get to see the X-rays, but they said it didn't hit a bone, which I knew.

I get flashbacks. I began thinking: What if? What if I had had one more traffic light that stopped me? What if I had been going a little slower? What if I hadn't been adjusting the radio; what would have happened then? It might have passed between the two seats.

That's the sad thing about it. Something like this can come out of the blue and totally fuck up your life. The cops came while I was at the hospital, and the guy was telling me how he'd worn his vest ever since he had a little girl. They asked me questions about where did it happen, what time, and he's writing these notes down. I said, "Loie, we're statistics." Also I was taking out credit cards and giving them to her. I said, "If I should pass out or they take me upstairs to operate on me, I don't want to be pickpocketed or have my shit raided." It's like some biblical den of thieves.

You can't blame the police in a way. It's such a shot in the goddamn dark. If there was some miracle to it all, I suppose they might have asked the questions that a friend of mine asked on the phone yesterday. How far did it enter? If it's a .38, has anybody ever done tests on how far a .38 penetrates into human flesh at a certain distance?

It's the randomness of it, the whole thing was random. You just take a tiny piece of the puzzle and say, this is a totally random fuck-up. This is something out of the blue. Then you realize that the only thing out of the blue is that I was there to catch it. I'm sure there's a certain precise logic that follows all the way to whoever sold the gun or whatever the circumstances surrounding why he had to have a gun, if it was some high school kid who had to have it for his own protection, a dope dealer, somebody who just wanted a gun, somebody showing somebody they could shoot, somebody handing somebody a gun and it goes off, whatever the circumstances were.

And also to have shitty luck and good luck at the same time. To have what could have been the worst happen and it's not that bad. But it's ugly to feel the pain and see the blood coming out of the hole. It's about two inches down from the crease of the elbow—with your palm extended upwards and your arm out, it's on the right fleshy side of the forearm.

I wasn't all that happy with St. Vincent's, so I asked this surgeon that I knew and he recommended a surgeon at New York Hospital. He did a sonogram and looked at the X-rays, and he was very cheery and airy and sunny about it all, and he said that I was healing well and that it might cause more harm ultimately to get it out than to leave it in. So I went and got a second opinion and of course it was diametrically opposed. I'm in a quandary.

Two things I want to hold onto about this gunshot. All my life, for whatever reason, maybe because I was second son, it plagued me that I wasn't a perfect person, that there were things wrong with me, that I was at best an 80-percent person. Which is a pretty good percentage, really, when you look at it. But when do you, as a human being, have a right to say, "I've paid my dues— I've had my share of suffering, deprivation, bullshit, lies, and now violence"?

It's not everybody that can boast that they've been shot. A nice middle-class kid, he doesn't get to know things that the guys who work down at the corner gas station know. Those guys, they got married early, they had their own cars, they smoked cigarettes, they were *guys*. And the nice middle-class kid was going to matriculate and stuff, and there was always this vague feeling that you didn't have street chops. So I thought, I'm going to give myself an honorary fucking badge that says, Mr. Street Okay.

And the other thing is, why should I hold in abeyance things that I want in life, or things that I feel I should say to people, for some other time, when I'm not sure there's going to be another time? Why not just sling it out there? The horrible part about it would be if it weren't for any goddamn reason at all, if you couldn't make any purpose out of it. It would be just too depressing.

Marshall Ephron, who's a wonderful humorist, satirist, writer—my best friend—I called him from the hospital and he said, "You ought to get on the phone and call the news services." He said, "Doesn't it make you mad?" I said, "No, it doesn't make me mad. I'm just glad that it's not worse." He said, "Don't you think people should know?" He is not a naive guy. He's a smart guy and he's got his share of cynicism about things, and he thought people ought to know that it's not safe to go down the West Side Highway. I called WCBS the next morning and they asked me when it happened. When I said "last night" they said, "It's not news." I said, "It's not news because a lot of people get shot on the West Side Highway? Or is it not news because only one guy got shot on the West Side Highway? Maybe other people get shot on the West Side Highway. How do you know it's not the beginning of a series of things?"

Through Marshall the [New York] *Daily News* got interested, then it hit the AP. WPIX ran a real nice thing on it, and it got picked up by the *Albuquerque Journal* and in California. I got a call from Michael Chiklis, who is the star of "The Commish," who said, "Jesus Christ, I saw you a couple days ago and now you've been shot."

I felt bad for the city, too. I came back from Vancouver—I had nine days of working in a lead there on "The Commish" series—and it was very civil there. I had the feeling that people not only didn't say "fuck you," they didn't even think it. I came back to see the Chrysler Building from the airplane, thinking, "That's my city, that's my city." The cab drops me off to pick up my car to go to the country. The cab stops and four or five guys in the car behind, instead of just going around, they're honking, yelling "fuck you!" Just crazoid behavior. Lot of hostility there. Two days later, after peace and quiet and watching bunny rabbits and stuff, you drive down and get a .38 in the arm.

That's fucking frightening. You struggle all your life to find meaning for things, to find connections, to respect nature, to respect the essential genius of life, and some fucking moron . . .

The arrogance, the audacity, the fucking arrogance of that!

A seasoned actor, Barton Heyman appeared in The Exorcist, Bang the Drum Slowly, Billy Bathgate, Bonfire of the Vanities, Awakenings, Incident in Baltimore *(with Walter Matthau), and other films, plays, and television shows.*

Steve Pendleton

I WAS ONE OF THE FOUNDERS OF ABATE, WHICH WAS fighting the motorcycle helmet law in Florida. I'd been to court that day against the helmet law. I had on a nice shirt, nice pair of pants, my court-going clothes. And I had a big old stack of paperwork.

I came walking out in the middle of the day, down University Avenue, which is the main drag in Gainesville, a four-lane highway, and there's this old black guy walking down the road in front of me. He's walking along, a shuffle-foot type guy, carrying a paper bag. There's a Salvation Army there that's taken over an old church. It's not like a bad neighborhood or anything, but it's right on the edge of one. This guy was walking, and I went to walk around him.

When I went to walk around him I got onto the grass and there was some dried leaves there, and I'm walking through it. I'm pissed off because I just lost in court. I come walking around and this guy all of a sudden turns around and starts screaming, "What the fuck are you doing sneaking up on me?"

I said, "You talking to me?"

He said, "Fuckin' A I'm talking to you," and starts yelling at me. And I said, "Fuck you, nigger, get away from me."

He said, "You don't call me no nigger!"

I said, "Fuck you, just get away from me."

He said, "I'll kill you, motherfucker!" And he pulls out a knife, a steak knife, with a serrated-edge blade. I'll never forget looking at it because most of the serration had been sharpened off of it, so it was real thin.

He pulled it out and I said, "Oh, motherfucker, get away from me," and I kicked him. I kicked him right in the chest.

When I kicked him, he didn't really move. I'd taken karate for a few years and worked out on the street for a few years. I'm a pretty good fighter. When I kicked him he didn't go down, so I kicked him again. And he still didn't go down. When I kicked him the third time, he came in on me and I heard a rip and I felt my chest kind of pull, and I said, "You son of a . . . "

I was going to say, "You son of a bitch, you ripped my shirt." I looked down and there was blood pouring straight out of my chest. My shirt was open—it was a snap-front shirt, like a cowboy shirt—and it was torn. Blood was coming straight out of my chest and hitting three feet in front of me. I felt like someone had pulled the plug on me. I felt like a balloon with the air being let out. I saw this guy was going to stab me again, and it was then I realized I'd been stabbed. I didn't even know I'd been stabbed. I screamed something about "you cut me," something like that, and I hit him with this whole big thing of papers I had in my hand. I mean I just hit him in the face with it, and then I ran.

I started to run to my house because I knew I was hurt and I only lived a block or two away. Then I realized I wasn't going to make it. I was hurting bad. I had an inch-long cut in my chest and I was bleeding real, real bad. I went about 15 steps toward my house and I realized I was never going to make it. So I turned and ran out into traffic. It was the middle of the day.

I got out in traffic and the cars were stopping like a half a block away from me. Nobody would come up to me, and the few cars that did, I ran up to them and they rolled up their windows. This one carload of old ladies, I know I probably scared them to death. I ran up and bled all over their car asking them for help, and they just drove away from me.

I started turning like in a circle. I saw a car come around the corner with another black guy in it, and the guy [that stabbed me] waved him down and jumped in the car.

Everything was going into real weird colors. I was seeing some cool colors, but it wasn't very cool at the time. I started kind of losing it.

I saw this guy coming up in a little station wagon on the wrong side of the road. Traffic was stopped, and he had to go around. He comes screaming up in this little car, and I was on the passenger side of it. He shoved the door open and he's yelling, "You're hurt bad, get in the car!" I got in and said I needed a hospital. He said, "I'll take you, but I don't know where it is. Tell me where it is." It turned out this guy was a medic in Vietnam. The stabbing was in '81, and Gainesville is a big central area for the VA, it's got a huge veteran's hospital there, and one of the largest psychiatric units for all the guys that are fucked up from being over there.

He was going down the wrong side of the road. I was directing him how to get there and I'd start going black, and he'd shake me or yell at me or whatever and I just kept coming back. It was maybe four or five miles through town to the hospital. It had been at least 15 minutes since I'd been stabbed. We got to the emergency room and he says, "I'll get a gurney." I said no.

My dad used to be a moonshiner, and when they were moonshining they had two drivers. The first driver would be a blocker and the second guy would be the runner. The runner would have the moonshine with him. If the cops came out or anything like that, the blocker would block the cop and let the runner get on by. That used to be a saying of my dad's: "I'll block, you run." That's what I told the guy: "You block, I'll run." He thought I was talking football stuff.

We went in the emergency room. I knew the emergency room really well, so instead of going over toward the desks or anything I just started in. I got through one set of double doors and I knew if I got through the other set of double doors that was where the doctors and nurses and all the real help was.

I was still walking alone. I was covered with blood from my chest all the way down. I had a set of tie-up boots on and I had blood all the way down into my boots. I wasn't bleeding any more. I had no blood pressure, no pulse. I was totally blue. The doors about this time opened up, and this black guy came walking out with a red smock on and a stethoscope, and I knew that a red smock was an emergency room doctor. Like I said, I know the emergency room *real* well there. And so I just fell into this guy's arms. I knocked him and me both, not down, but he kind of lowered me to the ground, and I looked up at him and I said, "Don't let me die." He said, "I won't." And he stayed right there with me through the whole operation, just locked eye to eye with me.

They got me up—by this time there were people around me—they kind of lifted me onto a table that was right there, off the hallway to the emergency room, and started ripping my clothes off.

They tried compressing the wound in my chest and it started suffocating me. By this time my lung had collapsed and I was starting to drown on blood. I told them this, and they were starting to freak out. They'd hit the code button already. The code lights were flashing and everything, and this doctor came running in.

I was still wide awake. I was talking to them up to a point where I couldn't move my jaw anymore because of lack of moving blood. My systems were starting to shut down. This doctor got on top of me and straddled me. This was another doctor who had come out of the cafeteria—he was having lunch—a little short redneck guy who's also one of the best heart surgeons on the east coast. He happened to be having lunch at the hospital where all this was going on. One day every six months he puts in as a volunteer emergency room heart doctor. He jumped on my chest and he told them to give him a scalpel. A nurse said, "Sir, I have to recommend that you don't do anything here. This isn't a sterile atmosphere."

I'll never forget that. I remembered it later on and they couldn't believe that I remembered it. But she had to warn him that it was unsterile to be entering into my body cavity in that area. He said, "I don't care," and they handed him a scalpel and right there in front of everybody he cut my chest open the rest of the way around underneath my armpit following my ribs. Then the nurse put this thing, it looked like a Volkswagen valve spring compressor, but it was actually a rib spreader, underneath my arm and in between my ribs and she said, "I'm sorry, this is going to hurt." And she broke four of my ribs in one shot. Then she put it over by my sternum and she broke the four ribs there. They pulled two one way and two the other and opened me up like a trapdoor.

The doctors cut some more and they took my lung out and set my lung in a nurse's hands—still attached. She was holding the lung, and the doctor put his hand down in my chest and plugged the hole in my heart, which was a half-inch hole. The whole end of the knife went into my right ventricle. He plugged my heart up and pumped it by hand, and they put two quarts in me. I had none. It's in the medical report, no blood pressure, no pulse. The only drug they'd given me at this time was some curare drug, two grains of that or something, enough to where I was completely paralyzed.

About this time the crash team finally got there, the heart attack guys. At this point was where things went weird, because I was seeing things from a different perspective. I don't know what, where, but I saw things from different views. Sometimes I was on the table. I saw everything that was going on in the room, but I don't know if that was because my eyes were wide open. Long about this time was when I shit myself and was pissing myself. That's what was really upsetting me.

Then all of a sudden I quit worrying. That was the one thing I remember when I died, was that I quit worrying. I was worried about my mom, I was worried about the bill— I mean, I'm watching all this major shit happening to my chest right there in front of me, I'm watching my chest open up and the doctors and nurses all around me and I'm naked lying on a fucking table not even in an operating room. I mean I'm just lying on a table. It actually was a cast-setting room is what it was.

They finished sewing my heart up, they closed my chest, got my lung reinflated, and I remember them looking all around it, looking for nicks. Are there any cuts in my lung? They found a nick, but no cut, so they got me reinflated, they set all the ribs in my chest. Actually they just set them there, literally, because they figured with everything happening they were going to have to reopen my chest because of infection. They just knew they were going to have to do it. Nobody was wearing a mask in the whole room, no gloves, nothing. I mean, he would have done it with a pocketknife if he'd had to.

This was a method developed in Korea for emergency open heart surgery. Whenever you have things intruding into the heart it causes fibrillation. About this time I went into fibrillation. My heart was beating a million miles a minute and not doing anything. So they started trying to electroshock me. The only problem was that I was in the cast-setting room and the machine that they had was meant for an operating room that has a special plug-in. And they couldn't find the special plug-in. I'll never forget the doctor just knocking the gauze bandage cabinet, just grabbing it and throwing it, because that's where the plug-in was. Then I'm black for a second or two. I don't know if that was the shock that caused it or what, but the next thing I felt was me landing on the fucking table and it hurt. It was like being asleep and waking up just as you hit a table. They hit me twice. I woke up on the second one just as I was hitting the table, *whack*, like a sack of shit landing. Then they said, "Okay, Steve, we're going to let you go back to sleep. You made it." I don't know if they gave me a shot or gas, I was pretty out by then. And I woke up in the elevator about an hour later, and about an hour after that I was in a room. Ten days later I was out of the hospital.

When I woke up I felt like I was inside a television set, I had so many wires, dials, gauges. I couldn't cough without an alarm going off. I had this great respiratory therapist [who] stayed by my side because I was total touch and go for three days. Even though they'd sewed me back up and everything was okay, I was still a hurting puppy. I'd lost all my blood, my heart was ready to go into an attack at any minute.

I'd just had major trauma to my chest. The whole operation took less than 26 minutes, from the time they entered my chest to the time they were done. In fact, on one of the "M.A.S.H." segments, Hawkeye gets pissed off at this new young heart surgeon who's going to tell them how to do it, and they describe the exact operation in detail of what they did to me. The doctor that worked on me was in a M.A.S.H. unit in Korea.

My lungs kept filling up, and that one lung especially. This respiratory therapist, every 30 minutes he had to take a tube—I was totally intubated, they were breathing for me, doing everything for me—and run it into my lungs and vacuum out my lungs. It's very, very painful for the person it's happening to. Greg understood this, and he stayed with me for 36 hours, vacuuming out my lungs every 30 minutes. He knew exactly how to do it, and I knew exactly how he was going to do it. My lungs would involuntarily reflex, and it would have killed me to cough, the way my chest was still lying open. They only closed it with eight stitches because they figured they were going to have to go back in.

Finally after 36 hours he left. But he was still in the building, and the first guy that tried to vacuum out my lungs hurt me so bad that all my monitors went off and I nearly had another heart attack. Greg came up and stayed *another* 24 hours until I was out of intensive care. He stayed right beside me the whole time. Every 30 minutes they'd wake him up and he'd vacuum out my lungs. Then after two days they made me get up. I was still attached and still had things down in my lungs and everything else, but they made me get up. The second worst thing was when they took out the breathing apparatus. When they take that out you don't know how to breathe anymore. Your reflex action's gone. You have to learn all about breathing again. If you lose the reflex of it, you have to mentally make it work. You won't just breathe.

At that point I couldn't move any of my body. The curare drug, when it goes into you, it settles into the muscle tissue and it paralyzes the muscle tissue. The only way you can get it out of the muscle tissue is by moving the muscles. It'll just lie there, but if you move the muscles it'll flow out. When I first woke up I was totally paralyzed—just lay there and blink my eyes when I had enough morphine. That was it.

I could move my fingers, and they had the bed with the sides on it. So I started using my fingers to walk up the bed rail, and that got my hands to move, which got my arms to move, and I just worked it like that, crawling up the little rails, and eventually it made all the muscles move.

To this day I cannot get around knives, even though right now I'm charged with supposedly stabbing a guy.

The last thing I would ever do is pull a knife on some-body in a fight. With my luck they'd take it away from me and stab me with it. And I'll *never* get stabbed again. When people play with knives in front of me I get really, really nervous.

Steve Pendleton is a biker. The easy-talking Florida native now resides in New York.

Bundy

JUNE 24, OKAY? ME AND MY BROTHER SAM—WE CALLED
him Stinky, his real name was Sam—we're going up the
block, right? He tells me, "Hey, Bundy, let's go up the block
and get a sandwich and a beer." We go up Arthur Avenue,
and one of his friends, I forget his name, was getting jumped
by six Dominican guys. I didn't know the guy, but he was a
friend of Sam's. Sam jumps in, and at the time I was a
prospect and I jump in. We started whaling these guys, man,
we were kicking their asses. I was beating up on three guys at
the same time.

Suddenly this guy, man, Sam whacked him once,
punched him right dead center in the face and busted his
whole nose up, you know? He's struggling with this other
guy toward the entrance of this building, right there on
Arthur, and the guy pulls out a .38—a .38, I think it was a
Police Special—and puts the gun right into Sam's side and
shoots. Sam got shot, and he had his blade on him. He
whipped out his blade and stabbed the guy in his stomach.
Stabbed him, *boom*, you know, and collapsed inside the
building. So while I was fighting this guy, beating the shit
out of him, I saw the gunshot get fired off, *boom*, and I look
and Sam's collapsing. So I'm running toward this guy, this
Dominican guy, and he looks at me and he shoots me. I got

caught right here in the socket bone, right underneath the hip. The bullet is still lodged in there.

And I didn't feel it, you know? I got even madder. I'm charging against this guy again—I wanted to kill this guy, you know? He pointed the gun at me and he clicked it, but nothing fired. When I reacted, I said, "Oh shit, let me turn around and duck." While I was turning he shoots me again, *boom*. And that bullet right now is lodged between the nerves of the spine.

But hey, I still hopped! I got shot and I hopped like half the block. Fucking blood is pouring out of my back like a fucking fountain. I couldn't take it no more so I collapsed on the floor. I'm saying, *"Damn, fuck man, I got shot! What the fuck, man!"* Fucking motherfucker, man, he gets up, right, he runs toward me and points the pistol right in my face, you know? When he did that I said, "Oh, I'm dead. This guy's ready to take my head off." And when he cocked it back, man, it was really wild because at that moment the cops pulled up. There were like 20 cop cars all over the place. And he's noticed the cops, right? So he runs back into his building and the cops are surrounding it and everything. The cops catch him inside the building.

My brothers came down, man, all my brothers were there, man. The officer was all right, the police thing that was happening. The only thing they could say was, "Hey, guys, we're here now, we'll take care of the problem, you know?"

We were driven to Jacobi Hospital down the Pelham Parkway. Everybody that gets shot, they go there, for shotgun wounds and shit. I'm on the fucking table, and they have me strapped down, and the nurse says, "We don't have any time. We're going to have to put your leg in traction. We don't have time to give you anesthesia or anything like that."

I said, "Well, go for it. Just do what you gotta do." Well, I said the wrong thing, man. They fucking put this pin, you know the pin when they have you in traction? They drilled it right through my leg. And I see this coming out and the fucking straps are ready to break. All the blood is coming out and shit. Fifteen minutes passed and my sister, my older sister, came down. I wasn't going to see her because she found out the news that I got shot and she couldn't face it. She comes down, and she's there, and she starts psyching me up, I'm doing okay, I'm doing okay.

So I told her, "Go ask the nurse what happened to my brother Sam." My sister comes back 20 minutes later and I say, "Oh, what's up? He's doing all right?"

She said, "He passed away." They tried operating on him and they couldn't save his life because that motherfucker, when he plunged the gun inside hm, he blew off the main vein that pumps right over here on the side. The main vein there, right? The bullet went through that vein and all that blood spilled inside of him. So he bled internally and they couldn't save him, man.

When I heard that, and I'm not fucking bullshitting what I say right now. They had me strapped down and I broke those straps. When I broke the straps I couldn't move that much and I fucking fell with the whole fucking bed and everything down on the floor, I was so pissed off. I was swinging up on the doctors, man, because I couldn't believe that, you know? One minute you see him, we're fighting, we're doing good, the next minute you find out he's dead.

But like I said, like I tell everybody, it's all right. I kicked the Grim Reaper's ass. This time. Kicked his ass, man. But to this day it's unbelievable. I go to the hospital and see my doctor every two weeks. He says where that shell is at, where that bullet is at, you're supposed to be crippled. That's from the one in the back.

There was another guy, he was right next to me, and he was shot in the back. The bullet was near, in almost the same spot where my bullet was at, and he wasn't walking. I was in the hospital for close to three and a half months. The first two months I couldn't feel my legs at all. I thought I was going to be crippled from the waist down. The real funny thing, the nurse used to come in and give me this shot in my leg for the prevention of blood clots. I was used to it already, not feeling the needle, you know? One day during the third month she says, "Hey, it's time for your needle." She started goofing with me, "It's not going to hurt, you know it's not going to hurt." I said, "That's right, it's not going to hurt." Because I don't feel the shit. So when that nurse put that needle inside me and I felt it, man, I said "Alright! I can feel that!" She says, "Really? Really?" And she runs and gets the doctor.

The doctor takes these little pins and inserts them in parts of the foot and says, "Can you feel this?" I said, "Yeah, I'm feeling it, doctor." So they rushed me upstairs for some more X-rays, and they brought me back and they noticed that the bullet was still in the same spot. And after that it took me about four more weeks and I started walking. I started moving the leg little by little. And then, in the fourth month I started walking again.

It's an experience, man (laughs). If I started riding again, my doctor told me I gotta have all the cushion, all the support I can get. He told me if you ride you gotta wear one of those weightlifting belts to support your back. Because if you don't and you go into a spill or something and you go down, you might get crippled because of that bullet.

But that's about it. Only when it gets cold it bothers, you know? I gotta pop these 800 milligram fucking pills, you know, eat about three of those. Motrins. Sometimes they work, sometimes they don't. Sometimes when it's cold I can't get out of bed, because it freezes, that spot right there where the other bullet is, in the hip. Like it gets locked there, so I gotta stay in bed. But when it's nice out, it doesn't bother me. The only other time it really bothers me is when I walk a lot. [The electric blanket] really doesn't help, man. In my clubhouse we have heat there, but it's still cold, you know? I have an electric blanket, but I want to get one of those heating pads. When it's real cold I can put that on and go to sleep, so the next morning, if I have to get up, I can.

That's basically what it is. I'm not a racist, I'm not a racist at all. But when it comes to Dominican people . . . you have to know these people the way I know these people. They're backstabbers, you know, they even kill their own brothers and sisters. You can't trust them, that's the bottom line. You can't trust these people. They're fucking money hungry. Those motherfuckers are starving in their country, and they go from their country to Puerto Rico to come here. And they put us down. Here the only thing they can do is sell drugs and drive a gypsy cab.

But I would like to see this motherfucker again. I know I would recognize the guy that shot me. I got a good look at his ass, man, it's like this picture right in my mind, you know? He might not remember me.

I lost a lot of weight. When I got shot I weighed about 265. The doctor told me that my weight saved me also. He told me that it didn't hit anything internally, you know, it just went right through the muscle tissue. In the hospital I lost 70 pounds. Then when I got back out all my brothers were looking at me like, "Bundy? That's you? Man! Got on that Slimfast diet?" Now I weigh about 240, so it's there, it's up there.

Bundy is a member of the Ching-A-Lings Motorcycle Club, Nomad Chapter.

Sharona Arikawa

DECEMBER THE THIRD, 1981, LONG BEACH, CALIFORNIA. About 7 o'clock in the evening, it was still kind of light outside. It wasn't pitch-black night. It still wasn't dark with stars all over, because I remember when they took me out to the ambulance the sky wasn't black yet.

It was somebody I didn't know. I think now . . . back then there was a lot of street gangs in the area, but because there wasn't so much publicity you didn't really know what a street gang looked like. Now that I think about it he was wearing gang colors. He had the plaid shirt and a bandanna tied around his face. So it was a gang member, and he had somebody waiting outside in the car.

He had been checking the place out about an hour before. That's how they got a description, because somebody had seen him. He had the gun in like a garbage bag. I guess he had looked in the window. I remember I was making dinner and I felt like somebody was watching me and I put the blind down. It must have been him.

The door was unlocked, which was really stupid, but it was still light. My sister was staying with me, she was like two doors down. My boyfriend's brother was manager of the apartments so we were always running back and forth, back and forth, right? So he just opened the door, kicked it open, and said, "Freeze!"

The gun was cocked, he cocked it as he came in. It was a .30-30 rifle.

So he kicked open the door and he said like, "Freeze!" My first thought was that it was a joke, you know? And then I said, no, it's not a joke. And he cocked it, I could hear it go *click*. Oh, God, I'm never going to get out of here, right?

So then he made us—my boyfriend was there too—he made us lie face down. My boyfriend was on the floor, I was on the couch. And then he went through our wallets and stuff. My boyfriend was a student at a diving school, he was studying to be a commercial diver, and I was working part-time in a restaurant. This was downtown Long Beach, which was not exactly a high-rent area anyway, right? So between us I think he found like $20.

So he started, "Where's the rest of it, you gotta have more, you gotta have more," and started going like really crazy. I remembered there was some money in the bedroom, so I told him, "I know where there's some more money." He told my boyfriend, "Okay, she's gonna come with me to get it. If you move, she's dead." Right? So I went down, I got the money, and he had the gun to the back of my head the whole time. As I was getting the money, I was in the bedroom, he said, "You know what I'm going to do to you now, bitch? You know what I'm going to do to you now, bitch?" He says, "Get over there," and he's trying to throw me over onto the bed and I thought, "Well, I'm never going to live [through] that one, right? So why go through it? Because he's going to kill me after anyway, right?" So I said to him, "I know where there's more money," and started walking out of the room.

Then he got freaked out because I'd kind of taken off, and he grabbed me by the hair and started to pull me around and I saw the gun there and I just pulled it down and it went off.

It shot me; it was right on my leg when it went off, but it's better than my head. What happened was the bullet went right through my leg into my boyfriend. It broke up into fragments and got him in the knee. As soon as I went down I was screaming because it hurt, right? Then he cocked the gun again, he was going to shoot me again. But my boyfriend felt like he'd been shot, so he got up. Cause he's still okay.

He must have had just two [bullets]. I'm screaming. My boyfriend's up, and he's bigger than him. He was going back and forth from one to another, like, who am I going to shoot? And that just cost too much time, so he got out of there. The best part was he dropped all the money when he left. That was the funniest thing; he dropped the money. He was really cool about it, though; he walked out of the door and just kind of kicked it, and he dropped the money, which I thought was funny after I got a sense of humor back, and said, "Aw shit," like, I really messed this up.

When the bullet hit my bone it smashed on impact. When my sister went to clean out the place she said there was blood in every room in the house. It was awful. So my boyfriend just got like fragments in his knee. He was fine. He missed like one week of dive school.

I was in traction from when it happened until some time in February, then I was in the hospital for one more month or so. It took an inch and a half of bone out, but almost all of it grew back. The doctor said he could put his fist through my leg.

Since then I've had one restructuring. It was fairly successful, but you always expect it to be better than it ends up being. The doctors told me I'd always have to wear those funny built-up shoes, and I'd probably never dance again, and I'd probably always have a limp, right? This was in March they told me this. Don't ever tell me what I'm going to do. In July I opened a new dance show.

I had acupuncture. I had to stay on crutches for a

while, but I used to swim every day, go to the gym. I'd do choreography and stuff for my dance show. Then I came off the crutches in the middle of June, and we opened the show like Fourth of July or something like that.

The only time I ever get any pain, it's never in my leg, it's always in my back, and it's from standing in one place. I could never work in a retail store where I had to stand all day. I did a thing with perfumes, Giorgio and stuff, and I couldn't do that, my back hurt too much. Dancing is fine. I can't run, but I never could so it doesn't make any difference. I walk from here [42nd Street, NYC] to the Village all the time. I can do everything I did before. Everything. Been dancing since it happened. And I dance athletically, right?

I went back to Australia a couple weeks after I got out of the hospital because they have free medical care back there. And plus, they'll do acupuncture, they'll do chiropractory, they're a lot more open. The American doctor was telling me all this stuff, and I would call up and tell my mom, and she'd go to the family doctor. Before I even went back he's studying my case, but studying it from a homeopathic view as well, a combination. So when I got back he said, "Well, let's try acupuncture."

The [assailant] died. He got shot in a police shootout three nights later. I got shot on a Thursday, and it was a Monday night. He, and I guess the guy that had been waiting before, they were in a stolen car. The police pulled them over and told them to get out of the car. He got out of the car with the gun, and they said throw down your weapon and he didn't and they killed him. They said they think he had been responsible for several break-ins and a shooting in the area, and I think the ballistics matched up and the descriptions matched up, so they were 90-percent sure it was the same guy.

[As a stripper/dancer, Sharona is often asked about her scar, which is high on her thigh and fairly large.] We made up all these stories all the time—sharks, crocodiles, crazed tigers—because I just got sick of telling the story. People are always asking. You can tell the story a hundred times, and it's no easier. I think there's a lot of rudeness involved. I always try to be polite, and then they always say, "Oh, I'm sorry, I shouldn't have asked." Then why did you? Are you that curious? Ask somebody else. That's what all my girlfriends in San Francisco used to do: "Well, what's the story this week?" and then [they'd] make up one, and they'd be telling people all these tall stories. It was kind of a protection for me.

I've never been refused a job over it. I don't think I lose any money out of it. I always get good bookings, good clubs. But I did lose out on some modeling and "Magnum P.I." I could have gotten a part on "Magnum P.I." I've missed out on stuff like that with it. Modeling and acting I lost out on.

Sharona Arikawa is a native of Australia and a career exotic dancer who currently lives and works in New York City.

Critter

THIS WAS IN A SEASIDE COMMUNITY. EVEN BACK THEN I had a reputation for being a hardass. If something got funky, call me in. This was like 1976 or 1977.

I was always doing my own stuff, moving weed, but I got called in occasionally for free-lance work. I was being called in as muscle, but I was also being called in as a carrier now and then. I'd carry for a percentage. And the muscle, people would be going into something like, hey, I ain't really sure about this, can you come with?

Back then I was really into carrying concealed weapons, something I've long gotten past, because I discovered something: you can't get to a concealed weapon fast enough. What I used to do, I carried these cheap fishing knives. You could go to Thrifty Drugstore and pick them up for 29 cents, and they had an unfinished wooden handle so they wouldn't take fingerprints. I was making sheaths by taking cardboard and sliding the blade in between the leaves of cardboard. Then I'd tape the sheath somewhere like the upper part of my arm in my armpit, or on my pants leg. I normally carried two or three weapons, because of not being able to get to concealed weapons in time. And when the shit goes down you'll be in some weird-ass position. So I learned to carry knives and razors in various parts of my clothing.

I got a call from this dude who I'd done some business with. He said, "Hey, I got a deal set up with this guy, and I'm not sure about this. I don't know this guy. Come with me, I want some protection."

We talked about it, and it was was one of those "his older brother knew a guy who knew a guy" deals, right? This guy was from the north side.

This was for a pound, and we were 17 years old. Five hundred dollars. Five hundred bucks was a shitload of money. That shows you how long ago it was, a pound of weed was worth 500 bucks. So my friend has the money, and we were going to meet this guy in an alley behind a school.

We go down there. I'm talking to my friend, "You don't know who this dude is, you've just talked to him on the phone," and it began to sound flakier and flakier. We got down into this alley, we're standing there waiting for this guy. We're supposed to meet him in this apartment building that has a laundry room. The deal's going to go down in this laundry room.

This guy shows up and I don't like him from the fuckin' start. He's a greasy-assed dude. He was older than us, maybe 20, 21, and he was already strung out. I'm looking at this dude and all my batwaves go off. There's something wrong here. He's carrying a brown paper bag, and I'm looking at it, and it doesn't look like it has anything in it.

Anytime that shit went down or was about to go down, I had learned that you don't go head-to-head with these people, right? I was always good for hitting from behind, which was why a lot of people really weren't comfortable about me. I moved back, and I'm watching this, and my partner's talking to this guy, and the guy's giving these evasive answers, and he wants to see the money. My partner wants to see the dope.

Like I said, this guy wasn't playing with a full deck, and he wasn't paying attention to the fact that I had drifted back behind him. I'm leaning up against the wall with my arms crossed. I had the knife up underneath my arm in my armpit, and it was hidden under my T-shirt sleeve. This guy is getting more and more tense, and I'm thinking, this is seriously fucking wrong here.

This guy's wearing an open jacket, and he says, "Let's see the money." My partner shows him the money and says, "Let's see the dope." The guys says, "I don't think so, man," and he reaches back. I see him move, and he's got a gun tucked over his butt and he starts pulling out his gun.

As he does this I pull my knife out in my right hand and I body-checked this dude. When I hit him I slammed the knife into his right side. Nailed his kidney. I shoved him across the room, and he dropped his gun, the gun flew out of his hand.

I'd seen all these movies. I'm expecting this guy to fall down immediately after I shank him. This dude stumbles over, he takes maybe two steps, goes down to his knees, and gets back up. And I'm thinking, *Oh, fuck*. Buddy, you're supposed to fall down when I shank you.

My buddy screams, "Run!" and he bolts out the door. I'm looking at this dude who's spinning around, and he's bleeding all over every fucking place now. He looks at me and realizes that I'm the one who shanked him. He's got his hand back now, and I'm thinking, *Uh oh*, so I drop the knife and just haul ass.

I'm cutting down the alley, my partner and I are running together. We get about 20 yards and we hear *blam blam blam*, and this guy starts popping caps at us. I thought we'd been running fast before. I'm hearing the bumblebee of the bullets going by. My partner and I split up—he cut through someone's backyard and I ran between two apartment buildings. Just hauled ass. I was about two blocks away, I'd gotten far enough so I could slow down. I figured the fucker was not going to come running after us because he walked up to where we were, so either he didn't drive or he left his car somewhere.

I'm trying to keep it cool. Part of me is saying, "Okay, I'm a bad dude now, I got to casually walk out of here." Once I got control of myself enough to know not to attract the attention of the cops, that's when it hit me. I got about five steps down the line and blew my groceries all over everything. I had the shakes, man, I was so fucking scared. I cut between two more apartment buildings and hid behind a Dumpster and just fucking shook. Here I am, a 17-year-old kid, I just shanked somebody, and he tried to kill me by shooting at me, and I'm freaking out. Oh my God, I could have killed this guy and he's going to come after me.

Then I began to think about the cops. I'm having all these fantasies about the cops beating on my door going, "You stabbed this dude," and dragging me off in handcuffs. And on top of everything else, I have this hard-on. I'm sitting there, and I'm so fucking horny, and like, this is not the time. Half of me is terrified, and the other half wants to go get my brains fucked out. I didn't realize it at the time, but that's a normal reaction.

That was the first time I shanked somebody. The guy lived. Even though I nicked his kidney, I hadn't hit him proper in a lethal spot. I found out that he'd been blown away in another drug deal a couple years later.

That's why I went out and started studying knife fighting: I shanked the guy and he didn't go down. Something's wrong here. Then I found out you gotta stab people in certain places before it's effective. You can shank somebody three or four times, but if you don't hit anything vital, the guy will be in the hospital for a while but the odds are he won't die. Had I known then what I know now, the guy would have been dead. It wasn't through lack of intent that I didn't kill this guy, it was lack of skill. I saw a gun, he was in the process of drawing a gun, and I went batshit. I was so scared that I had to kill him. I had to kill him to stay alive.

It took me a long time to settle with the fact that I'd stabbed somebody. Up to this point it had been a game. It wasn't until later when another buddy of mine got killed in my front room that it really 100 percent became clear to me that it wasn't a game. I was excited, I was giddy, all these things were passing through my mind. I was horrified one moment and then totally elated that I was still alive, and then so horny that I'd fuck a snake if they'd put it in a sundress. All these things at high speed. I'd stabbed somebody, and it was horrible, but I'd come out okay.

Too many people think this is fun shit, and it's not. You get these people who think it's a game to go out and kick the shit out of somebody, and as long as there's four of them kicking the shit out of one guy they think it's ha-ha fun. Never mind that to the one guy it's not fun. Then these people get upset when they come up against that one guy and he pulls a gun and blows one of their buddies away. Like, "Well, that ain't fair." Like four against one is fair?

Like I said, even after I shanked the guy I had the vestiges of believing it was a game. I wasn't sure what to think about myself for a while, because part of me was ready to shift into, "Hey, I'm a bad dude," versus another part of me that was repulsed by the whole thing.

Critter is a California chameleon and attracted to the good life. Now you see him at the unemployment office, now you don't. Watch your back around him.

Big Steve Trinkaus

THE SCENE IS NYACK, NEW YORK. NYACK IS A RIVER town on the Hudson, near the Tappan Zee Bridge. It was Main Street, a bar called Blondie's Cafe, and a friend of mine was playing blues there.

On Main Street, all the buildings used to be houses, but now they're stores. The facades aren't facades, they're truly old houses. It's an odd town. First of all, there's total civil upheaval. There's no more Nyack police. They killed the police department and now the town of Clarksdale is the Nyack police also, so the cops just don't give a damn about anything. They resent having to go there. And there's a lot happening. It's lively in the street, very commercial. Across the street from Blondie's, one side is all old houses that are now cafes or stores, and there's a movie theater and a two-level shopping plaza. The lower level is actually sunken down, you walk down maybe 10 steps from the street. I don't know why they did that, but that's the way it is. There's concrete planters, and a lot of people can hide down there. There's a lot of crack going on, right in front of the cinema. Guys piped up like you wouldn't believe, going crazy. Their eyes move independently.

Blondie's facade is equal proportions of front windows on either side of the door, which is in the center. In front of each front window is maybe a three-by-three or four-by-four section of porch. There was a full front porch, but they cut it away for the entrance. It's beautiful. You can stand out there with a drink and they don't say anything. They sometimes have a table or chair out there to make it look quaint.

Red Tyler was the bluesman, and I was standing out on the porch with his manager, this guy named Steve. We were getting some air. It was 11 P.M., and there was nothing unusual about this night. It wasn't Friday the thirteenth, it wasn't Halloween or cabbage night, whatever you want to call it. We're just talking, nobody else around.

And we hear a hissing and we hear a bump-bump, like coming off the porch roof. What? We looked down, and about three feet away was this stick of dynamite. Both of us gazed at it. I couldn't believe the size of the fuze. I remember having M-80s and blockbusters on the Fourth of July and tying them to rocks and sinking them and blowing up fish, all that juvenile shit. I was amazed. I'd never seen an explosive that big. It wasn't tremendous, but it wasn't any blockbuster, or pineapple, as they call them, which are quarter sticks of dynamite. I've seen all the street fireworks, and it was nothing like that. But it still had a fuze that you light, and dynamite is all done with caps. So I don't really understand, but I guess you could make one.

Just for a split second I was real interested in looking. Like, wow, look at the size of that thing. It must have been the same with Steve too, right? Then we looked at each other. No shit, I'm not trying to add any drama to this—not until our eyes met did we realize, man, we better get out of there.

Maybe the instinct would have been to jump over the railing, which is not easy for me to do at 300-plus pounds, and kick it out of the way or something. Briefly that was in my mind, or I would have left faster.

Steve is big, tall, and gawky. Me, being so big, I'm used

to being in people's way so I always try consciously to be courteous about it. Like standing in doorways—you shouldn't. It's not like if people bump into me I stare them down and start fights. That's not my forte, you know? However, that instinct is still there to get out of his way.

So he stumbled over some fucking table they had there to make it look quaint. It wasn't even functional. If you sat down, you'd have no room, you know? So I grabbed him and threw him through the door. Nothing really heroic, but the words weren't there, and my grabbing him made him realize: you first. There wasn't time for discussion. Just from the grabbing motion he realized I was going to let him go first. It wasn't like I picked him up from the jaws of a shark or something.

The door is maybe 4 1/2 feet from where the thing landed. It may have rolled a foot or so, it's hard to tell from the actual blast site on the concrete. And I don't know if they blast perfect center or what. So Steve was down and I caught most of the shock.

The music stopped. The people in the bar rose to their feet. Not a single window shattered, and it's all fucking window. That's what's so weird. The door was open and the back door was open. The cops said sometimes there's venting or something. I don't know. But I know what I felt. Maybe it's fat and overweight flab is sensitive. It was like someone took an oak plank and beat me. That's all I felt, a constant sting. You could have cut me with a knife after the sting was there and I wouldn't have felt it. The sting over-rode everything.

I stumbled. We were both down. He stumbled and like skidded on his knees, and I just fell flat on my face and looked like a total fool because I'm just not in shape to do some Olympic skating move, you know?

The sting to the back of my legs and my ass was just so strong. I got up slowly, like I meant to do that kind of stunt, you know? More embarrassed that I fell on my face than anything else. I started very slowly feeling the backs of my legs, which had no feeling but that sting. I couldn't even feel the pressure of my hands. But I was feeling for wetness, for blood. And I was almost afraid to put my hands out to look. It hurt so bad, and it continued hurting for a good hour. I went in the bathroom and dropped my pants and found that the pressure had actually split the skin. Flab is more sensitive than toned muscle. Pressure splits, there were two of them, one on the back of each knee—lower thigh, right by the knee. That area, it's really soft. My pants were not damaged at all, anywhere. It was just the force. I still have discoloration; it never healed. I mean, they can inject you pneumatically, you can get inoculations just using air pressure. They don't even use needles. So I can imagine with something like [a bomb].

I went back out. We did not see where this came from. It was like it came from God. It came from above us. We didn't see any cars drive by, nothing. Just came out of total nowhere. But across the street in black man's crack land they made an arrest. A white guy. Looked like a typical guy who was all worked up and pissed off about something. Turned out that his old lady was fucking around on him with a biker type. He threw another stick of dynamite into an open window at his old lady's house that night, and then came down and went on the rampage. There was talk that he was trying to get it in the front door, which like I said was open, propped open, no screen or nothing.

The other guy that was with me looks like a biker. He's not, but he looks the part just coincidentally. He looked like either a biker or one of the Grateful Dead. Long hair in a ponytail. That was enough for this guy, with his short hair—looked like an ex-serviceman with a beer belly, no job, five o'clock shadow, the whole bit. You get the type. He looked like the kind of guy who was something in the service but never ever had anything going for him when he got out. Just got drunk, and his old lady fucked around.

They arrested him, right? Cops didn't even come over to the fucking bar. And the bar had called the police. I didn't, the other guy didn't. So I go outside. I was still sort of like in shock, but I was more mad than curious. I was definitely awake. I said to the cop, "You don't want to talk to me about this?" They didn't want anything to do with it. The Clarksdale police, they resent even being in Nyack because they have to work twice as hard in an even shittier section than they're used to. And I can see that.

The cop didn't even seem interested. He said, "Well, are you hurt?" And I said, yes and no. I don't think I have to go to the hospital or nothing, but what the fuck, you're arresting the guy.

All the time I was talking to the cop there was some fucking spade standing on the upper level of the crack hideaway, the two-level shopping center next to the movie theater. He was wearing a big black and white shirt, real flashy, and he kept waving at me. The cops says, "Ah, they're all piped up, fuckin' niggers." Little white guy, about 45, balding, about Archie Bunker's build. Looked like he wanted nothing to do with life, much less being a cop in Clarksdale and working in Nyack. He says, "Well, if you want to come down and file a complaint you can, but we got him on other things and you'll never get anything out of him." This and that. I realized he was probably right, although I resented his attitude about it. What's the difference if somebody throws a stick of dynamite at you and it doesn't hurt you and if they shoot at you and miss? There was something in my mind telling me I should have followed through on this, but they said I would have gotten nothing out of it. I mean, the cop has no legal authority to make a decision like that, or a consultation. That's for the lawyers or something. But at that point I just deemed the whole situation unbelievable, got disgusted, and let it go.

I'm standing there about an hour later, still calming down. My friends weren't going to let me ride home until

they were sure, for their own conscience, that I was okay. I
knew I was okay, but they wanted to make sure I could
stand, that I wasn't drinking, the whole bit.

Now, the fucking nigger in the black and white shirt
comes across the street. He was around the area where the
white guy was arrested and dragged in. He comes over and
he just smelled of doing time. And sure enough I was right.
I found out later he'd just gotten out of the joint. He was
with some young guy wearing a "Bo Knows Your Sister"
shirt. Another black guy. He's about 6 foot. They're both
ripped to shreds, independent eye movement and stuff—
they were both piped up and crazy.

I'm not bad. Let's get that straight. I'm not bad. I'm all
right, but I'm not bad. And I never dealt with no niggers. I
didn't have nothing on me. I was wearing my painting
pants, the ones with the hole in the pocket, so I never put
my knife in there. Plus I don't like going around New York
state with weapons because they're real tough about that,
especially if you're a Jersey boy. There's a thing there. I
usually carry my butterfly. I don't drink beer, so I didn't
even have a bottle in my hand. They started getting in my
face, saying, "Don't ever do that again," saying they were
gonna fuck me up. I didn't have nothing on me and I didn't
have anyone to depend on. Next thing I know he's moving
up his shirt and there's a pearl-handle—either a straight
razor or a little pistol. I couldn't see which.

He was about 35, but his friend was about 21 or something, really, really muscular, and repeating everything he
said, like:

"Gonna fuck you up!"
"Gonna fuck you up!"
"Two times!"
"Two times!"

Shit like that. I said, "What the fuck are you talking
about?" I was getting on with them, but I wasn't pushing, I
wasn't moving forward. I never felt so helpless and frus-

trated. I had nothing. I do not like straight razors. Guns I'm not fond of either. And I'm in no shape to deal with two crack guys. I mean, these guys were strung out, they were going crazy.

I never filed a report, but it turned out that [the bomber] was a friend of theirs, and while he was being arrested they were saying that I was the one that got him in trouble and was fucking his old lady. None of it was true; I never knew the guy. They told me if I ever came around there again I'm not going to be able to walk away and all this. I'm having a bad night.

Finally they just left. And I'm standing there, I don't believe this. That got me more upset than anything else.

The guy's away for a million years, which means he'll be out in two, and I went back there with a bunch of the boys but never saw the niggers again, so they're probably dead or in jail already. But there's a whole new batch, which is nice.

Big Steve Trinkaus is a biker, builder, and ceramic artist. He lives in Northern New Jersey.

Carl Karstetter

I WAS WORKING WITH A TEAM, I WAS MARINE CORPS attached to the Fifth Special Forces Group in Vietnam. I worked from the upper part of I Corps into Laos and North Vietnam.

We had a stand-down, we weren't doing much of anything around the firebase. Place was called Thor; very few people have heard of that place. Jungle penetrators, they have a stabo rig, they drop you down and you hook up to it—they're long ropes, everybody hooks themselves together. Well, four Special Forces that came back were dead, and so was the guy they tried to kidnap, an officer in the NVA. Four more were still stuck in this LZ [called Quebec] so they mounted us up and we went into the LZ. It was very early in the morning. Just sunup, five thirty, quarter of six, something like that, we went out. We were supposed to set up the perimeter; 32 of us set the perimeter and that was it. Do the extraction and go.

Well, what they thought was a small group turned out to be two battalions of NVA. We were there for 20-some hours, and 11 of us came out. I didn't get scratched. After all that. I was on the last lift out. We got the bodies in, we got the people in. I jumped in, the bird took off. I emptied my rifle, sat down, started to shake, threw up . . . I was just a total vegetable lying on the floor.

I was in the hospital for about a week, being fed, I really couldn't do anything. They wouldn't let me go out on any more long-range patrols. The newbies coming in the country, we would just train them and work them around Da Nang for the last couple weeks. That was pretty much the way that went. I didn't get involved in any more contact like that.

I got back in 1967. 1972, I'm minding my own business down in Lancaster County, Pennsylvania, on a farm. We hunt this farm year in and year out for ringnecks. In Pennsylvania you're not allowed to walk standing corn. So we skirt this standing corn and we didn't see anything. It's raining, it's the first day of the season. It had been raining pretty heavy during the day and it was misting. At that time I smoked, and we were standing in a semicircle discussing what we were going to do.

I had my shotgun curled across my arms and my hat pulled down. It was a little windy, and I tried to strike a match and light a cigarette. And I'm lying on my back. It didn't take the feet out from underneath me, but it hit me behind the legs and on the upper thighs. I just went down, *splash*.

I knew instantly what had happened. I'd been shot. There was no pain yet, no stinging, no nothing. I just went down. He had accidentally shot me.

I rolled over and here's this guy, you know, the classic scene, a little wisp of smoke from the gun barrel . . . So I shot him. I hit him three times. I popped him three good times. I had number 7 1/2s, relatively small shot, and I hit him mainly in the face and chest. Didn't do much to his chest, but it screwed up his face a little bit. I rolled over and was reloading number two magnums, which I used to carry for geese. Large, substantial shot size.

One of the guys who was standing directly in front of me, his name was Tony Fisher, he didn't get hit, he jumps on my back: "You're trying to kill that guy!" Well, first and foremost in my mind was to return fire and suppress that individual. All my training, all my experience, just went on automatic mode. I knew the gun was empty, I knew I hit him each time, and I was just reloading until he wasn't gonna get up again.

Meanwhile, Leon, who was a relative of the guy who owned the farm, he was hit. Actually, he was hit the worst because he got grazing wounds, which cut across the skin and require more stitches. It was fortunate that the shot was big. Shot does not carry the ballistics of a solid projectile. It decelerates very rapidly but transfers the energy quickly. Whatever time elapsed between when I was hit and the pain set in, it could be equated to being hit by a big, flat board. A stinging sensation. Wow. It's like when you get slapped with a flat board on wet skin, you know the pain is going to go away, but boy, it's really taking its time. This *didn't* go away, and it's in a place where you can't sit well or maneuver, no matter what you do. The butt and the back of my legs. And especially the tendons in the back of my knee. Those tendons weren't penetrated, but they were swollen from the shot itself.

Not as many pellets penetrated as I initially thought. I just looked and said, "Oh God." It was raining, and there was a lot of blood, and the water tends to make it look a lot worse than it really is. Leon seemed to be hurt the worst. Again, he got the grazing end of it.

The guy who shot us went back to his car. I'm upset, I'm hurting. Tony pretty much has everything under control. He was the adult there, he was the controlling factor. He gathered up everybody's guns so they wouldn't shoot anybody again. Three of us were hit. The third individual, he didn't have any penetration. There were mainly big welts. We found out later we were fortunate that [the pellets] were as large as they were. If they had been smaller shot, like I was using, it would have penetrated through our fabric faster and would have penetrated the skin easier. The only problem we had was that the fabric was drawn in with the shot.

I think I got a half dozen to a dozen still left inside. They have been coming to the surface over the years. You just kind of dig around with 'em and pick and pick and you can bring them out.

In the emergency room—that was a weird thing, the emergency room. I was very fortunate as the one pellet went right across the inseam [of my trousers] and cut the inseam, or it would have taken part of my scrotum. That was the only thing that scared me afterwards: my God, too close to my credentials. It was the classic scene, hang over the table and as they take the shot out you hear them drop in the pan, *tink*. We were being questioned by, well, the state troopers were there, of course, and the game commission was there, and they all have their reports to fill out.

The [guy who shot me was] lying next to me, we were separated by a hanging sheet. I was pretty belligerent in those days, that was before I had therapy. He made a statement, "Well, I shot my brother last year and *he* didn't get mad." And that pissed me off. This triggered something. I pulled his gurney over and went to hit him. And the state cop grabbed me, and literally, the man had me hanging off the ground. As I went to swing he just snatched me up like a baby and threw me up against the wall. I immediately sirred him to death. I weighed 180, 190 pounds at that time, and if he could keep me off the ground, all right, no problem.

I called the VA right away and told them what happened, tried to go the flashback routine. They sent lawyers up and filled out statements, and so on and so forth. What happened was that I lost my [hunting] license in Pennsylvania for the rest of the year and was on probation for the next five years. The shooting, they went with the conditioning because of the war. [The guy who shot me] lost his license in Pennsylvania totally for the rest of his life. It was fortunate it was like it was and not deer season.

Scuba instructor, gunsmith, workout fanatic, Carl Karstetter was in a state of heavy life flux when this interview was conducted.

Eddy

I WAS LIKE 14 YEARS OLD, AND I GREW UP IN DETROIT. Cass Corridor. It was predominantly black. It was kind of a drug thing, but not really. I was a total idiot, obsessed with white power, a skinhead. I was really into that. A total idiot. I smoked a lot of angel dust.

I sold drugs, too. There was this dude from my same block and he didn't like that I sold drugs. His friend came up from behind and stabbed me a couple times. I was on the ground and I felt the throbbing in my lower back. It was pretty gnarly. I bugged out, but I wasn't hurt at all—I mean really hurt. I was scared shitless, freaking out, and the only people that were there were the guys that stabbed me.

I laid there and pretended not to be conscious, and they left. Then I got up and ran my ass off to my friend's house. We went to the Detroit emergency room where I sat for five hours and waited until the doctor came. When he came he fixed me up and sent me out. The guy who stabbed me was another kid, and it was really, really dumb. He could just as easily have knocked me in the back of the head.

It was like another lifetime ago. I just wasn't that good at [being a white-power skinhead]. I wasn't very good at it.

I guess I finally figured that out. Plus, I came to California and learned that a lot of things weren't the way I perceived them to be. Detroit is a different reality than the rest of the world. It's in America, but it's not how most people perceive to be what Americans live like. It's like Beirut. It's nuts. There's no work, no nothing. It's totally segregated and it's just not a happening place.

I got stabbed again in Youth Authority, Michigan YA. I kept hitchhiking to California and going back, coming here and going back. Coming to California was like the ultimate dream, you know? It was like a serious quest. In YA I had a fistfight, and the next day I got stabbed with the back of a kitchen utensil in the stomach. In fighting, no one ever does win. Even if you don't get hit you're beating the guy with your hands and your hands get all fucked up—unless you're in a movie and your hands don't ever get hurt. I know my hands, all my fingers have been broken about 20 times. I've broken every finger and every knuckle, I have arthritis and everything.

I definitely came out on the good end of the deal, because I probably stabbed 50 people. I carried brass knuckles with a blade that retracts, so you can keep it in your hand at all times, and I always wore them because I was little, you know? Some of these events were with other kids, but a lot of them were with adults. I had those on my hands at all times, just ready. I'd always fuck people up if I could, if I could catch them and get them right.

I'd punch them a few times, and if they went for something in their pocket I could just whip it out. That's how it started. Then it got to where I'd just beat them up and take the knife out and cut 'em up. Why not? That would really prove my point. There was no stopping me: you're going to get fucked up and you're going to have a huge scar. And that's all I cared about because I'd go nuts.

Then I came to California and I saw that it really wasn't that way, and people weren't out to get you. When I was in

Detroit I really felt that way, and I had a reason to. They almost really were, you know?

It's evil shit, drugs and stupid kids. In the '60s it was different, but when I was a kid in Detroit, it was dust and purple microdot mescaline.

Right now, heroin's in vogue. Now, everyone knows someone who's hooked on heroin, the same as a few years back everybody knew somebody that was hooked on crack, and before that everybody knew someone who was hooked on coke. Heroin's everywhere. I mean it's everywhere. I don't use it because I'm not a fool, and I like drugs. I always liked drugs, and I still do, and I'll always use them. Not a lot, but I do use them. I was a dope fiend, and kicking once was quite enough, thank you very much.

But if you're on dust and mescaline, you're an insane person. There's no question about it. And when you're a kid, and you're filled with all these ideas that are totally wrong—any idea. Any idea that you take to that limit, an extremist idea and a lot of drugs, and it's a bad fucking thing. Something's going to happen, and it's going to affect someone else.

Eddy is an artist who now makes his home in the San Francisco Bay area of California.

Joe Werner

GETTING SHOT WAS EASY. GOING TO THE HOSPITAL was the tough part. Really. The whole thing started, I came home Friday night, I had a couple dollars in my pocket, you know, looking for a place to go out. I was almost gonna stay home, but my mother calls me up and says, Jeff, a friend of my sister's old boyfriend, is having a birthday party up at the Woodcrest Bar. So I got ready, took my shower, got dressed, and went out to the bar. There was a private party in the back of the bar.

We were just hanging out, having a good time and having a few beers and stuff, and I go to the bathroom. Like I said, it was a private party in the back of the bar, and the front part was for the patrons or whatever. The party's going on, I go into the bathroom and do my thing, and I come out of the bathroom and there's like nobody left in the bar. Like, there's only a couple women left in the bar and everybody's like gone. It was all full before. I said, "What the hell happened, where'd everybody go?"

The bouncers were standing by the door and I said, oh, there must be a fight outside or something. So I walked outside the door. The bouncers weren't letting anyone else out, but for some strange reason they stepped aside for me and outside I went. I saw a friend of mine, Dean, that's Jeff's brother-in-law, and he just finished getting the shit kicked out of him.

After they beat him up—and they beat him up bloody bad—what appeared to happen, I was partying so hard I didn't notice what was going on, but these guys come in, these cardboard gangsters, they were like coke dealers from across the street. They came in and they went into the women's bathroom. They're doing their thing inside the women's bathroom and it got a little bit annoying. There was a line of girls outside waiting. So the guy, Dean, that got the shit kicked out of him, knocked on the door and said, "Yo, pal, how about it?" And a guy came out and called him outside.

They called him outside and all his boys were across the street and they just mobbed him. I was in the men's room as all of this was happening. When I came out, as I said, the bar was clear and I walk out the front door and they just got finished kicking the shit out of him. I saw them get the last kick in. And as they finished, the whole mob started walking by me. As they're walking by me, the smallest guy says, "Are you one of them?" By "them" I guess he meant the friends of the people he just beat up.

So I said, "Fuck you, punk, who's one of them?" And he took a swing at me, and me and him are at fisticuffs. I knocked him down and a second one came in and I got a good punch on him, a real square punch, and the second guy went down. After that there were like four other guys with bats and shit, and I was getting hit with bats and stuff, whatever else. It was just a bunch of flashes of light.

All of a sudden the flashes stopped and I'm up and still fighting, going. I never went down. I didn't go down getting hit with the bats or nothing, and they must have got pissed off that I didn't go down. The second guy that

I put down, he got back up. When he got back up I see him go into his pants—he's wearing a sweatsuit, just picture a typical guinea in a sweatsuit, fuckin' wiseass—and he goes into his pants and pulls out the gun. And the only thing I could think of when I saw the gun was, "I'm not gonna get shot in the ass."

So I said, "Go ahead, punk!" *Boom*, I seen the flash come out of the gun and I yelled, "Ya fuckin' missed me!" and I started running after him. He started running away and he's shooting over his shoulder.

As I'm running after him my sister's seen that I'd gotten hit, so she grabbed onto the back of me and says, "Stop fighting, you were shot!"

I said, "No, he missed me! He missed me!" I looked and it was right underneath my neck, it happened right where the two collarbones come together. I looked down and I didn't see no blood, then I saw a little drop of blood. I ripped my T-shirt off and I still couldn't see nothing, and then I started feeling this aching pain on my side. "Wow, you must be right, I must be shot."

As all this was going on these guys were running across the street, jumping in the car, popping caps across the street, a couple guys I was with were popping caps back, and after that I just went into the corner and waited for the ambulance to come.

A police officer came up to me. It was a woman police officer, and I started getting really stupid with her and everything, but she was real good, trying to keep me out of shock. I was being real fucking obnoxious with the cop, I guess, you know, but she was good. She didn't take offense. So the ambulance came and I was gonna be Mr. Tough Guy and I wouldn't let 'em put me on a gurney and I walked into the fuckin' ambulance and they took me away.

When we got to the hospital, that's when the tough shit started happening. I wanted a pillow so bad because my back was going into spasms real hard because of the pain and everything. Now, when he shot me, the bullet went in where my two collarbones come together, went by my esophagus, by my jugular, into my back, and somehow must have gotten turned and went down through my lung, through my diaphragm, and stopped just as it touched my liver. And that's where the bullet sits now, right there. And it had to have hit all soft tissue because you can see it's perfect. I'm just kind of hoping it's copper and not lead, but I don't really know what composition it is.

They were gonna go for it, but I said, "If there's any way you can leave it, leave it in because I don't want my chest spread open and a major scar in the middle of my chest." And recovery from a chest operation like that's tough. Not only that, but the bullet's closer to my back than it is to my front, so as they spread my chest they would have had to go through everything to get to the back. So they just said scar tissue would surround it and it should be held in place pretty much.

The funny part about this, my mother had a dream two days before that it happened. She had a dream that I was shot by one of my sister's ex-boyfriends and that she was right there and seen it happen and when she came over to see if I was okay, all I kept asking was, "Ma, I need a pillow, give me a pillow."

When I was in the hospital I told 'em I had a couple drinks so they wouldn't give me any medication. I figured, I'm not lying, I'm telling it straight out. So I told 'em I had a couple drinks and they wouldn't give me anything, and I sat there 24 hours until they were sure I was detoxed, as far as they were concerned. They wouldn't give me any pain-killers or anything; they were just doing tests and probing all night.

They took me right in and started doing all kinds of X-rays. I went to Jamaica Hospital, and they have the best trauma unit in the city. It was funny, the head doctor was a woman and she was real young too, like 25 years old. I almost punched her in the face when I went in there. They put a catheter in me; oh, man, I couldn't believe it. I don't think there's a worse pain, and I was fighting with 'em the whole way. That's a funny thing about doctors—they figure the bigger you are the less pain you feel. I'm six one, 225, 230. I was just giving 'em a hard time: "There's no way you're gonna stick that catheter in me. No way, no how." And she came up close: "You're gonna die, do you understand what I'm saying? You're gonna die." And she's in my face. I said, "Listen, I still got a free hand. You better back up if you wanna yell at me like this." Later on she did proceed to save my life, you know?

They had doctors and nurses, everybody running around like crazy, all for me. They took the X-ray, looked at the pix, and saw I was getting fluid in my lungs. So they had to drain the fluid. It looked like a 5/8-inch piece of copper tubing cut at an angle, and they stabbed me with it right through the rib cage and drained all that out. Again, no anesthesia, no nothing. Right through my lung. And that thing stayed in there for days.

I really got lucky. It happened Friday night, September 15, at like 12:01, just after midnight. It was the fourteenth when I went out and the fifteenth when I got shot. On Tuesday morning I was out of the hospital and I was riding my bike that afternoon. I got a '78 Sportster. I was kind of proud of that.

But I was still wheezing, too. For a long time after that I had fluid in my lungs. Even my old lady, in the middle of passion, would say, "Take it easy, take it easy." But it cleared up, I figured I'd work through it. I went to the doctors after that and said, "I've got trouble breathing." They basically said, "We can't get all the liquid out of your lungs, it's going to have to come out by itself." So it just cleared up after a couple weeks. I moved my girl-friend, she moved to the sixth floor in a building where the elevator was broken and that was only two weeks after I was out, so I was up and down the stairs. It was exercise like that that cleared me up instead of like sitting there doing breathing exercises.

I was shot 16 months ago. He was only standing—like I said, I knocked him down in the fight—and he was only standing about 8 feet away from me. It had to be a .25 automatic because I didn't see him pull back a hammer or nothing. From what I can remember, you know how your memory plays tricks, but from what I can remember it looked like a .25. The bullet size looks like that. That's what everyone was carrying, too. It definitely wasn't a .32.

The whole right side of my body underneath my arm where the bullet is now is kind of numb. It's kind of weird. It's not really pain, it's numbness that I feel. The funny thing is, after I was shot, when I first came home from the hospital, you know those touch lamps, you just touch them and they come on? The electricity from your skin is supposed to turn them on and off, like a sensor. I couldn't turn them on for months afterwards. It was months before I could turn them on. It weirded me out, I had to get people to turn the light on for me. That was about it though, the numbness in my chest and I couldn't turn the light on for a long time. Six months afterward I was pretty much 100 percent. I was high on life after I was shot. I was just so happy to be alive.

The X-ray is real clear. They said the bullet just touched the liver. It stopped as it touched it, and it didn't damage it at all. Look at all these X-rays. I've got five pounds of X-rays here.

I'm kind of what you'd call a thrill seeker anyway, and when I came back from being in the hospital a couple days, I couldn't buy myself a drink. *Couldn't buy myself a drink*. I didn't get get shot in this bar, I got shot on Atlantic Avenue, but everybody knew in the neighborhood that I'd got shot. People thought I was dead, there were stories that I was dead, people were crying at home and shit. They thought if he got shot he's gotta be dead. I come home and people see me walking into a bar a few days after I get shot and I was Mr. Celebrity. I had stories to tell and drinks to drink for nothing. So it turned out to be a positive thing. It's another story to tell my grandkids, you know?

You don't have to be right, you just have to protect yourself. Even if you're dead wrong. Just recently I had a fight. With a drunken fool, we went out to pick up some beers and he said something stupid to this woman and her husband was right there and chased after us. This was just a couple of weeks ago. After we pull out the guy follows us. There's four of us in a van, we were all drunk, and one of the guys was getting out of hand, one of the guys I was with.

So he chased after us: "You wanna fuck with my old lady? You wanna fuck with my old lady?" We pulled over and showed him there was four of us there and there were only two guys in the other car. He didn't give a shit, he wanted a part of all of us. So he reaches under the seat and one of the guys goes, "He's got a gun!" So we jump back in the van, take off again, hit a red light and traffic, and there was nowhere to go. I was in the back of the van, and the driver says, "Listen, the guys are out of the car, it's do or die!" So boom, we jump out. Not for nothing, I was wrong. The people I was with were wrong. But this guy, he didn't give a shit, he's out there with a razor cutting everybody up. I had my plunger knife and I stabbed him three times in the side and he went down. It was real fucking close.

But the experience I learned was, I don't give a shit if I'm right or wrong, I'm not gonna be on the bottom side of the pile anymore. Never again. Those are the words that I say: never again.

Joe Werner lives in the Bronx. He played football in high school and college and was voted high school MVP two years in a row as a center and defensive tackle.

Pepsi

RECENTLY, APRIL ELEVENTH LAST YEAR, I WAS WALKING down the street with my wife. At the time she was five months pregnant. Five thirty in the afternoon, busy street, a lot of people on the street. This was Spanish Harlem, 110th Street and Third Avenue. It's busy around that time. The train station's on Lexington, that's one block over.

I was just walking down the street and there was these young kids, they were about 16, 17, 18. There was about five of them. They were riding bicycles, like those small dirt bikes, riding them on the sidewalk, and it's crowded. They were bumping people with their bikes like it was a joke. As they got up to me, ready to hit me and my wife, I just put my foot out in front of the bike like, hey, you know? They were all black, American black. I says, "Hey, say excuse me or something, you know. You can't just be riding on the sidewalk hitting people with the bike."

At this point one of the guys, he was 15, 16, says, "Do you have a problem?" I said, "I don't have a problem. You have the problem. You're the one riding on the sidewalk bumping people with the bike, you know?"

I was ready to just leave it alone, then another guy came over and he asks what happened. I told him what happened and he said, "So what?" Then a few more guys come behind him. At the same time my wife is pulling me, "Come on, let's go." We had to go shopping, take care of things.

I said, okay, let's forget it. Me, I always try to look out for a brother, especially a young brother, like hey, it doesn't have to be like this. But this day I learned my lesson. That doesn't work with these kids nowadays.

I was about to walk away, and the guy that asked me what happened punched me in the face. Snuck me, you know, as I was about to walk away. So I let my wife's hand go and started fighting them.

The funny thing is, nowadays kids can't fight. They're so busy trying to profile and style and get nice clothes and valuable things—looking good—they don't really practice streetfighting, sparring. You know, like when we were kids you did that. They don't do that nowadays, so they really don't know how to fight, they just have the anger in them. And if there's more than one of them they have a lot of anger. So I started fighting them, and funny thing, I was beating them up. Catch one, *bang*, one run around me, catch one, *bang*.

So they started this pattern. I would go to one, and another would hit me in the back. My adrenaline was going, I was up. My wife stepped in, like hey, you're jumping him. All these people were around watching it like it was an entertainment show. They can see my wife is pregnant, standing there, and no one helps me, you know?

I just got so upset I grabbed one of them and tried to break his neck. I was *so* upset. The rest of them jumped on my back and got me to the floor. While I was on the floor I was still beating these guys. They were trying to hold me down and I grabbed one leg and *bang*, and *bang* the other one, kick the other one.

One of them got tired of this. They were looking embarrassed, with five guys on one guy [and me] beating them up. So one guy got tired and he pulled out a box cutter and sliced my head—cut my head open here [left side, just above the scalp line], gave me 30 stitches. After he sliced my head another guy came behind me with a pipe and hit me with a pipe in my head.

That just got me madder, you know what I'm saying? I got up—I thought I was just hit with the pipe, I didn't feel the razor blade cut—I got up and one of the guys had left a bike on the side. I said, "Fuck this, man, I'm gonna take this bike and give it to my little nephew, you know? You punks, man." And my wife says, "You're bleeding, you're bleeding! You have a lot of blood coming out of you."

I said, "Aw, it's just a little cut, you know." Then I saw it was pouring down and pouring down and that got me more upset. I said, "I'm gonna kill one of you little bastards." The crowd was still all around, they couldn't really just run out of the crowd. So I chased one of them, and he ran around, chased another and he ran around, and one of them, I cornered him off so he really had to fight me. I'm backing him up, about to get him, and as soon as I got his neck a cop came out of nowhere and grabbed me, ready to hit me with his stick. My wife screamed out, "He's the victim, he's the victim." They turn my face around and see all the blood and said, "Wow."

The cops arrested the guys, found the weapon, and used my wife as a witness. We had to go to court and whatever. Originally I wasn't going to press charges or nothing. I said, "Let 'em all out, let 'em go free. I'll take care of 'em. Forget the law system." My wife says, "You have to press charges in case something happens to them later." I said, okay, I'll go along with it, please my wife. And I pressed charges.

We went to court a couple times with these guys, and because I didn't spend the night in the hospital or die, all these kids got off scot-free. They all got off scot-free. So these same kids that got me are running around in the streets, starting trouble, looking for trouble, doing the same thing. The system just lets them go like that. It's terrible, terrible. Nowadays you have to pack because the system's not going to be there for you. Especially with younger kids, they get away so easy.

These guys, actually, they almost killed me. They had to rush me to the ambulance and when they got me to the hospital they didn't have time to give me anesthetic to numb the area, they just had to rush and push my head together and sew it up. No drug or nothing. That was painful, you know? But because I didn't die or stay in the hospital overnight, those guys got off.

When this happened, I was in the process of becoming a professional boxer. It happened April eleventh, right? I was in training, in the best shape of my life. I was in training for my pro debut as a middleweight. I was going to fight June first, some time around there. When it happened, I thought it wasn't that bad, the cut wasn't that bad, that I could still go at it. But I come to find out they cut an artery and really damaged my head up there. Wounds like this take sometimes a year, two years to heal. I'm just waiting for the doctor to give me the okay so I can maybe fight again.

It's the inside of my head that they're worried about. The cut, the blood could cause me to go into a coma or black out, just black out. It can cause brain damage, because the veins in there are messed up a little.

I've tested it already, did a little sparring since then. It didn't affect me, but I did feel a little sensitivity around the area. That's why I'm letting the hair grow longer, so I can have a little bit of shield there, so I can be more protected.

Actually, it did ruin my career. I was in very high spirits, about to become a professional fighter. I had a lot of promise ahead. It really damaged everything. Hopefully by this time of year I could have had seven, eight fights, hopefully undefeated, you know, working my way up. I would have been noticed by now. Maybe the latter part of this year I would have been up for a title shot. Hopefully. Depending on how impressively I'd done in my victories. I had it planned out, you know. This screwed everything up.

The guys that did this to me, they all had little records, you know, misdemeanors, doing drugs and things like that. Not too many assault charges or anything. Me, I don't have any type of record or anything like that. Just a simple guy, I got a family, a wife, I go to work every day. And they still let these guys go. And this is happening a lot, all over the city, especially with these box cutters. All the young kids between the ages of say 9 and 18, they all carry these box cutters, and that's not illegal. And these box cutters are very dangerous. They travel around and get into a little fight, the first thing they pull out is a box cutter. They don't think about taking the chance of fighting. They just use 'em *snap* like that . . . It's very easy to hide them.

These kids turn out to be monsters, monsters, and they're crazy. Something has to be done about it. At one time—my wife, she really talked me out of it—but at one time I was really serious about building myself back up, getting in some really good shape, and be like Spider Man. Go out at night and look for these types of incidents and rescue people and bring these guys to justice. I was really serious about this.

After this happened to me I went on a rampage, went out and got a gun, just so I could have something to protect myself, and I was really going to do it. I know a lot of areas where these things happen and these kids do these things, where they hang out. They all just look for trouble, everyday. They're looking for trouble. If they rob you and you got $10, it's not enough, they kill you. Or even if you have the amount they want they just kill you to kill you, so they won't have to see your face again and you won't see them again.

They're scared too, and they don't know how to handle

situations, so the best thing they know how to do is just kill 'em. They don't care. They could run into somebody who's very, very dangerous and that person . . . for instance me. If the cops wouldn't have came when they came, I would have killed that guy. I had his neck, and I would have just snapped his neck. I would have killed him. And I would have went to jail, I would have went to jail no questions asked. Even though they started the whole thing, I would have went to jail.

Pepsi lives in New York City.

Ron

MY LEFT KNEE IS MY ONLY PENETRATING BULLET WOUND. It was done with a .22-caliber hollowpoint. The worst thing about being shot in the knee wasn't so much the actual bullet but the aftereffects. It went in the left side—it was quick, but when you get shot, everything seems to happen in slow motion. Anything traumatic seems to happen in slow motion. I hate that slo-mo feeling because I can't stop the situation. It hit, I felt it, felt the knee going, I saw the stuff come out—that was bad, seeing the meat come out—and I hit the floor. It wasn't extreme pain, it was just numbness. The inside kind of burned, the powder burns, because it was close, maybe two feet. It was my mother that shot me. At the time I was 10, 10 1/2. That was the start of the severe abuse. From there things just got worse.

She's in Montana now. I keep tabs on where she's at because there's that lack of trust. She's pissed because she got sent to prison after I turned her in, both her and my stepfather. There's this vendetta. If she showed up I would try to kill her first, and vice versa. It's not a good situation for either of us.

As I got older I went into fighting karate tournaments and hurting people. I wanted to hurt people, that's why I did it.

Point fighting was my speed. I could hurt people and call it an accident. Full contact rocked my brains a little bit. My first fight was with some Filipino kid, and he clocked me so bad with his foot that I didn't know where I was or what was happening. I'd never hit anybody or been hit full contact. I had three fights and decided that it was not for me. I can do it in the streets and I can do it in the ring for points, but the sport fighting with the special kicks, I mean, I'm a streetfighter nine-tenths of the time, so forget it.

I went from that, and a friend of mine said, "Well, you can be a stand-in for me as a bodyguard." He was working for a company, and he told them, "Ron's good." They said they'd test me out.

I learn quick, and I react to everything that happens. There's that split-second thought, then I respond. They thought that was good, so whenever he got hurt I was a stand-in. This was in the Bay Area, San Francisco. I wouldn't do anything where I was living, which was in Sacramento, because I didn't want to get put in a position where I had to nail somebody whose brother or cousin remembers me. I've gone through that already, and it's not good. In some cases, people survive and go to prison, but you kill their partners and you're on their list when they get out.

I wanted to get into it because I thought I could be tough, I could be mean to people and get away with it. It was a legal way of taking out my aggressions. But being shot changed all that.

Pain. It was not so much the pain of being shot, but afterwards, like not being able to breathe. Not being able to take a full breath because your ribs are cracked. You wear the vest, which stops the bullet, but it doesn't stop anything else. People have a misconception about bulletproof vests. For the record, all they do is stop the metal fragment that comes at you. Everything that's behind that fragment comes through the vest, all that power.

I was shot with a .44, that's what cracked my sternum. He had me, I never drew my gun. My buddy was hit first and I spun. Why I spun without drawing first I don't know. I just spun and *bang.* I hit the roof of the car. I'm looking right at him and everything went out of focus. I guess I tried standing back up because he hit me again. My legs were going like I was riding a bicycle backwards. I hit the car, fell off, hit the ground, and heard my head hit—didn't feel it, just heard it.

The pain of being shot is humbling. It makes you think more, especially while you're recuperating. Lying there, I'd be thinking, well he didn't do a head shot, Lord knows he could have. He was right in front of me.

It made me feel more human. Up to that point I was not a feeling person. I was a badass, I thought I was a bad ass. I decided it was a no-win situation. Okay, I get 600 bucks out of this. Where's it going? I can't work at Roundtable now for a month or two until I can walk and function at a normal speed, so the money's got to keep me going until I feel better. Maybe I'll do it one more time and figure out what I want to do.

That time never materialized. I think I respect life more now. I'm not as quick to get in a fight, I'm not as quick to try and beat you down, even though I feel I could. Child abuse gave me a high tolerance for pain, it just never gave me the big picture, what happens afterwards.

I prefer being shot to being stabbed. When I got stabbed there was a burning sensation when the knife came out—not going in, it was coming out. I felt like somebody poured gas on me and lit a match. I wandered around for a while and passed out in front of the Presidio. That's where they found me. I had flipped off some Chinese guys. They were walking down the street in this big flock, and I was too cocky for my own good. I was way outnumbered. But there was no thought process, they called me something nigger and I just said,

"Fuck you." Then I thought, oops, maybe I shouldn't have said that.

Sacramento, I have to kind of stay out of there, because that's another situation. In my job as a Roundtable manager I was involved in violence on a daily basis in this one neighborhood. My attitude got pretty bad. There, people shot at me, but they always missed. Crips and Bloods, unless they get some kind of formal gun training, will never be formidable. The first time they shot at me, I walked out of the restaurant with one of my employees. The car pulled up, and I knew what was going to happen, and they started firing. He went prone, and me, I grabbed my keys and went for the door and then realized, "What the fuck am I doing here at the door? I can't get in!" I hit the ground and I'm crawling, and Alphonso said I looked so funny. But I'd never been cornered like that before.

After that, if they pulled up to shoot, I realized that the bullets were hitting up high. These guys are driving by, and the recoil takes the gun up, and they're shooting over my head all the time. We'd return fire, shoot the car. It got to the point where five of us were packing guns. It took a while for these guys to realize, yes, we're going to display our force. This is our restaurant. You can do what you want in the rest of the shopping center, because that's the way things are, but not in here. It wasn't until we shot this Impala—it was funny after it happened. The guys came in the restaurant and threatened us just before we closed. I hate when people threaten my female employees. It just totally pisses me off. I said, "Look guys, you got a problem, talk to me. I'm the manager."

"Fuck you."

"Well, you can't do that because I'm not your type." I was trying to joke to lighten it up, but I was getting mad. "Look, you have a problem with us, you might as well leave."

"Oh, we'll leave, but we'll be back."

I called a couple of guys who worked for me and told them to bring their pieces. So there's six of us. We waited until 11:30 and nothing happened. So I said, "Okay, guys, we can jam."

We walk out the door, and as soon as the door was locked and we were out there, they pulled up, no headlights. I didn't even say anything. Guns were out. The windshield was gone, tires went—I know we shot two for sure, because they were being carried off. The car was sitting maybe 50 yards from the front of the building. We pumped everything we had into it, dropped magazines, reloaded. They were all running away. The cops never came. The next morning we called them and said, "There's a car in our parking lot that's been shot up." After that we got respect.

Ron lives in California.

Ray Michaels

MY FATHER AND HIS FATHER RODE MOTORCYCLES. SO DO I. As a biker, I've lived on the fringes of the "outlaw" world all of my adult life, with occasional voyages deeper into some of the bizarre and often dangerous activities associated with the life-style.

I'm an ex-Marine, 6 feet 1 inch tall, and weigh in at 185 pounds. A journeyman iron worker by trade, I'm in pretty good shape.

I've always been fond of weapons, especially the medieval cutting weapons; my interest in the martial arts led me to become very proficient in using these weapons. I suppose it was only natural that, with my skill in metalwork, I would become a weapon-smith or maker of weapons. It was only a small step from making and using these weapons for fun to teaching others to use them. A marginally lucrative step.

My life has always been a paradox because of my love for weapons and martial arts with an almost phobic hatred of physical violence to other people. So I became a Marine, right? Beats me. I've always been perfectly capable of violence, and I have a hot temper, but I just never really cared for it, even though I've been deep in the middle of it way too many times. It seems like a contradiction of terms, eh? Kind of like "police intelligence."

Like most bikers, I've always loved to party. Not too often, since I'm a responsible kind of guy, but when I do, I party hardy. I tend to get amorous when I party, a trait that's led me into trouble on several occasions because, unfortunately, I tend to be far less rational and discriminating when I'm out in the ozone. I usually nibble on every female in reach. They generally don't mind, but it sure pisses off their husbands.

It was understandable, then, that I could get involved with a young lady who, I was quite sure, was underage. It didn't make any difference to me; she talked the talk and obviously wanted to play.

It was quite a shock when I found myself in jail, a week later, charged with rape. I was in some serious shit!

Since I had an inordinate amount of faith in the system, I figured that everything would turn out OK; justice would prevail and I'd be cut loose. The reality was, since I couldn't afford much justice, I was "made an example of," which just happened to translate into a bucketful of political brownie points.

I received a life sentence, with a ten-year minimum to be served before I could even think about a parole. Anyone wanna tell me exactly who got raped?

Because of my time structure, I was immediately sent to the maximum security prison after my sentencing. The security goons that formed the welcoming party were a real thrill, screaming commands in your ear and zapping anybody that blinked with a Taser. It was a relief, after all that, to be thrown in the hole (solitary confinement), where I could regroup and stop shaking.

My first cell assignment put me in with a guy who produced a razor knife after I told him why I was in prison and told me I had to move out of that cell. Wow, welcome to prison! I didn't think it was worth spilling blood over, so I moved. No big deal.

The next cell they assigned me to was empty, in a quieter housing unit. A much better arrangement! As I began to settle in, some of the other guys on the tier came by. Some extended warm greetings, while others tested me. I began to realize just how far out of my element I really was; this was like being in a foreign country, where I only spoke a few words of the local language. I was completely lost!

A biker named Moose had noticed the artwork I was doing on the envelopes I was sending out. He turned me on to more art supplies and got me set up doing artwork for other guys to support my tobacco and writing habit, since I had *no* income at the time. Moose tried to teach me to play pinochle too, but I never could get past seeing a royal flush with all those face cards in my hand. Life was improving.

Moose was the one who had shown me how to boil water for coffee hobo style by setting a wad of flaming toilet paper on the back of the toilet while dangling a can of water over it by a string. A primitive method, with one obvious drawback—it was *real* hard on the porcelain toilet. With a pop like a small-caliber rifle shot, the entire fixture split neatly in two and began to ooze water from the hairline crack.

Since I'd just moved in, Moose suggested that I go tell the unit cop that the shitter was broken when I got there. It sounded good to me since I didn't want to pay for it!

The housing unit was divided into three wings, each containing two tiers with a "recreational area" off to one side, halfway between the tiers. There was one cop in a control booth between wings watching closed-circuit cameras that monitored activity in the tiers. To get his attention, it was necessary to stand against a wall in the rec area, push a little red button, and shout into the speaker grill, knowing that *everyone* could hear the whole conversation. I played like a tourist: "Hi, I'd like to complain to the management . . ." The cop fell out of his chair laughing, but I got a new shitter the next day.

A week later, I was just beginning to learn the ways of my new world. I was surprised when I came back from seeing a law clerk about my appeal to find that I'd gotten a cell partner. I'd have to remember to thank the administration for letting me know. They were *so* considerate down there!

This guy seemed OK. Jack was as big as me, with a dark, sinister look, but he seemed to want to get along.

After two days of playing questions and answers, his attitude changed abruptly. He'd been out on the yard, talking to some of his "road-dogs" [buddies] to see what he could find out about me. As it turns out, the first cellie I'd had was one of his bros, who told him all about my passively moving out of the cell when I was told I wasn't welcome. That set the stage for the events to come.

My second cellie was an Aryan Warrior, but since he didn't have any of the usual racist tattoos, I hadn't recognized the warning signs. He perceived my response to his bro as showing weakness. When he heard about my charges, he became convinced that I would be an easy victim. He decided to test the theory that very afternoon.

Everyone had told me that cellies stick together and defend one another. No one had mentioned that one cellie might want to victimize the other, so I naively accepted his warm smile and friendly demeanor as he continued the questions we'd been tossing back and forth. In retrospect, I can see that I really should have noticed the coldness that crept into his voice when I told him that my second wife was a mixture of white, black, and Indian. A *very* unaryan combination!

Later, as I sat on my bunk writing a letter, Jack came into the cell and, without any warning, punched me in the head. I was stunned and saw stars, but reflexively defended myself with a couple of well-placed kicks that backed him off. We screamed at one another; he was using terms that I didn't understand at all, accusingly. When he saw that I had no idea what he was talking about, he apologized and we shook hands. I still didn't understand what we'd fought about, but it was done now; we were friends again.

A couple of hours later, as I continued working on the letter, trying to utilize the overhead fluorescent light to see by, Jack mentioned that the light hurt his eyes and asked if I could get by without it for awhile. The cell was arranged with the bunk against the outer wall, under the window. The guy on the top got plenty of natural light from the window and unobstructed light from the overhead, while the bottom bunk was like being in a cave.

I always try to be helpful and accommodating (I was a Boy Scout; I can't help it), and I like light, so I offered to switch beds. Mattresses were moving before the echo died! It made sense for me to move onto the top bunk, since I needed the light to write by and I didn't have many reasons to wander around the tier anyway. Once up there, I discovered the wide, deep windowsill and how groovy it was for setting all my writing and art supplies on. I was setl

That night, as I leaned over the edge of the top bunk to look at Jack while we talked, he gave the bottom of my mattress a little shove with his foot, sending me airborne. Taking a nose dive onto a concrete floor from atop a 5-foot bunk would fuck up most people, but not me. With a dazzling display of coordination, martial arts training, and *lots* of blind luck, I tucked, rolled, and came up standing in a defensive kung-fu stance, screaming obscenities. Jack was immediately apologetic, assuring me that he'd only been teasing me and hadn't meant for me to go flying. I was gullible—I believed it, but I didn't lean over the edge of the bunk anymore.

The next day, Moose, Jack, and two of his road dogs came into the cell and lit up several joints, passing them around. Good shit! As we sat around afterwards, toasted out of our skulls, the tall, wiry young moron (literally) that lived with one of the other guys came in. Having five guys in a 6- by 10-foot cell is cozy enough; we didn't need anymore bodies in there. When he decided he was gonna crawl up on my bunk and snuggle, I tweeked.

I pushed him back with a foot to the chest, telling him to fuck off. I repeated the procedure when he returned, giggling insanely. When he started to come back again, I hopped down to the floor between two pairs of knees and nailed him in the chest with a jump kick that knocked him completely out the door onto the tier floor. He was laughing wildly as he started to get up, but all hell broke loose right then, so I missed seeing him return. I was struck—hard—above the left ear and the lights went out.

Sometime later, I awoke to discover that I was being kicked in the ribs. When I tried to bring my arm up to block the kicks, someone stomped on my fingers, breaking two of them. The kicking stopped, but each breath was agonizing, like inhaling fire. Cracked and broken ribs. I looked to see who had been kicking me, only to find that I couldn't see; the world was a dark, fuzzy blur, with ghosts moving through it.

Someone turned my head roughly, pulling my hair, and tried to force something into my mouth. I bit something firm but yielding, right before my jaw was broken by another kick. The lights went out again.

When I came to again, the room was spinning, I was choking on something being forced into my throat, and someone was slapping my head, telling me not to puke. It sounded like the right thing to do, but the vomit never made it past the obstruction in my throat. I think I was on my stomach, with someone pulling my head up and down by my hair, doing a very good job of choking me to death.

I tried to pick out voices, desperately seeking some clue into what was happening around me, but I couldn't make out the voices through the roaring noise and blinding pain inside my head. It all fell into place as someone grabbed my hips, pulled me onto my knees, and forced something into my asshole—*I was being raped!*

I tried to move and got punched in the kidney, then passed out again. Time became a nightmare of being beaten, raped, and manipulated by threats and verbal degradation (that I "deserved" what was happening because of my crime).

The prison has a daily "health and welfare check" where every inmate is required to stand up at one of the head counts to prove he's healthy. During these, I was propped up against the bunk with a knife at my back to keep me quiet.

Someone was always with me. I could bearly walk—I kept falling over, from the head injury—and couldn't chew. I knew I needed medical help soon or I was gonna die.

After five or six days (I'm still not sure), my tormentors all went somewhere together, leaving me alone. I took the opportunity to stumble down to the wall speaker in the rec area and call for help.

At the infirmary, I was interrogated before I was allowed access to medical help. Security first! It was probably just as well, since the "medical treatment" consisted of a cursory visual inspection of my body for wounds, bruises, etc., and a very thorough rectal exam (looking for "evidence"). I was never X-rayed, even though the nurse noted—after I pointed it out to her—that I had a major concussion.

I spent three weeks in the infirmary, locked in an isolation cell, trying to make the best of a regular diet and aspirin. I never saw a doctor (I found out later that they didn't *have* one then) or received any actual treatment.

A classification counselor came by at the end of the third week to ask what I wanted to do. Well, after three weeks of quietly brooding (I wasn't allowed to talk to anyone), I'd made up my mind that I wanted *revenge*. I wanted to spill some blood!

I guess the counselor figured that out too, because I wound up in a heavy-max security lock-down cell to "think about my choice." The cell was eight by eight, with a single spring bed and a toilet. I had no mattress or bedding; I was only wearing a pair of torn-up jeans.

It didn't take long for me to figure out just how persuasive this situation could be. I had my choice between sleeping on bare springs or the cold concrete floor. One pinched and cut while the other sucked out my body heat. Fun!

Four days later I was sitting on the floor, shivering, when the counselor returned to see what I wanted to do. I was too tired to care where I went. I spent a year in protective custody, where I became depressed and suicidal.

It was mildly reassuring to find out a few months later that when all the crazy shit had gone down, Moose had beat feet and wasn't involved.

I got involved in the psychological therapy program after my transfer to the medium security prison. I was suffering from post-traumatic stress disorder; I'd dream of *slowly* shattering the bones of my tormentors with a steel bar (a Viet Cong trick), then wake up drenched in sweat, shaking, sometimes screaming.

After four years of intensive psych therapy and antidepressant medication, I've started to believe I can live with the memories.

Jack was in this yard awhile back on a parole violation. It was difficult for me, even though he didn't even remember who I was, until a couple of days before he left on parole again. The really hard part was the day before he left when I saw him on the phone, his back to me and completely unaware of the world. I stood there for over 20 minutes, weighing the alternatives: kill him now and never have the chance to leave prison, or walk away, thinking of the life I've begun to build with a woman who knows about all this, understands and accepts, supportively. The logical choice was obvious, but difficult.

It took several days for me to realize that by my choosing to let go of my desire for revenge, I had experienced a cleansing of sorts. I felt a great relief, knowing that I *could* have killed Jack but chose not to.

Ray Michaels is still in prison.

Jesse

I'M 26 NOW. I WAS 15 WHEN THIS HAPPENED. THIS WAS
in the Rocky Mountains. We were on a camping trip, me
and this guy, Bob. We went out to a place called Medicine
Bow National Forest, which is in Wyoming. He took his
bike out and I went along with his wife in a pickup truck. It
was about 60 miles from where we lived, which was in
Cheyenne, Wyoming. We went out to stay the weekend,
from Friday night to Monday morning.

We got pretty drunk on Friday night and we heard a
lot of weird noises going on. Just a lot of weird stuff.
Heard a baby crying, heard dogs yelping—but that could
also have been taken as coyotes or wolves too, because
you just never know.

It was kind of curious because it didn't sound like it
was all that far away. So we got some things together
and went for a little walk. We were walking through this
valley and we saw a big campfire. Huge campfire, like a
bonfire. We watched for a little bit to see what was going
on. We sat up there for probably about two hours. This
was from midnight, maybe 1 o'clock in the morning
until about 3 or 4. We watched these people and what
they were doing and stuff. As it turned out, these people
were devil worshippers. They were a satanic cult, and

they were doing religious sacrifices, and they had a baby.

We didn't know that at first, until after watching them for awhile. We had no idea. But we could see the dogs. They had several dogs, and they had one that was strung up on a tree that they had cut the back legs off. We had a pair of binoculars. Bob used to be in Vietnam, and he had all kinds of night vision stuff, infrared glasses, and that's what we were watching them with. We could see this dog was strung up on a tree and they had cut its back legs off, and they had cut its throat. It was bleeding, and they were dripping the blood into this pan.

We watched for awhile, and we were talking about what we were going to do—if we should do anything at all, of course. We waited and waited, and he thought the best thing we could do was wait until they went to sleep, if we were going to try and do anything—because his first thoughts and my first thoughts was to try and get that baby out of there.

It looked like as far as what they were doing to the animals that they were going to sacrifice this baby. That's just the impression we got from them. As best I could make out, they had their whole ritual kind of thing, with all these knives they laid out on the table, they got their robes and everything. These people were into it, heavily into it. We really had no idea. I was 15, this is basically my first experience with this. I'd heard of it before, but I'd never seen anything quite like this.

Bob, he got kind of irate about it, and he kind of wanted to take them out right there. But we decided that the best thing we could do was wait around. So we went back to our campsite, sat around for a little while, and talked about different things and what was going to be done and stuff like that. We went back over there, and these people had pretty much disembarked. Some of them had left, I guess, or they had spread out.

We snuck down into the camp and we took this baby. Just snatched the whole cradle. Bob ran in and snatched the whole cradle. And we took it back to the campsite. When we got back to the campsite, it started to get light out. At that point we went to start the truck and the truck wouldn't start. We were getting ready to split, you know? So we went to start the truck and the truck wouldn't start at all.

He's got this 750 Triumph that he was riding, so he got on that and went to go out. When he started to pull away a truck pulled in and blocked the road. So he turned the bike around and came back and parked the bike next to our truck. Judy was sitting there in the truck, with the baby. This pickup truck is a two-seater, old air force, with two full seats and four doors, a bed, the works. She's sitting in the back with this baby.

These people get out [of their truck] and they start walking toward us. I had a .22 semiautomatic rifle, a .25 automatic pistol, and Bob had a .30-06 and an AR-15. He also had a .357 that he shot .38s out of. I had never been in a situation like this before. Obviously Bob, being in Vietnam, knew exactly what was going on right away. He also had two live hand grenades. He started getting all his shit out. He laid his weapons right up on the truck to let these people know that he wasn't fucking around, there was just no way. And they knew it.

A couple shots were fired. There were some people walking out of the woods [behind them] and they all had rifles, as best as we could see. There was a helicopter that was flying around up above, and we suspected that it was the army or the air force, because the F.E. Warren Air Force Base is in Cheyenne, and they probably do a lot of maneuvers out there. So this helicopter is flying around overhead and we were trying to get their attention because we thought they could help us. If they would come down these people might disband.

They were walking toward us and Bob just told them, he yelled right out, "Anyone come any closer and I'm gonna start opening fire." He had this AR-15 that was converted. It was fully auto. He says, "You come any closer and I'm just gonna blow you away. I'll blow you away." At that time I was called Kid. I never had a dad, my old man left before I was born and this guy was my father figure, taught me how to hunt, camp, fish, all that shit. He always called me Kid, and he says, "Kid, get your gun." I didn't know what the hell he was talking about, and he said, "You know what I'm talking about, get that .22." It had a 15-round clip, and I had five or six clips anyway. I had a whole bunch of 'em. He said, "Get that and hang out by a wheel well." I remember him telling me to hang out by a wheel well, so I hung out by the back wheel well.

Those people, they stopped. The guy yells at him, "You got no business here." Bob said, "No business or not, what you're doing is wrong." They were yelling back and forth. "You're a bunch of fucking sickos," is what Bob was telling this guy, "You're a bunch of fucking sickos."

The guy goes," Yeah, yeah, yeah. You had no business interfering with it."

Bob goes, "Well fuck you," and he goes *dow dow dow* and let off three shots. They went into the ground in sequence about a foot apart. And he said, "Back off, motherfuckers." The guy stopped.

At that point somebody came out of the woods directly behind me. I got hit with an AR-15. The guy got right to the back of me, and I was standing there at the back of the wheel well by the truck. The guy came right up behind me, and I didn't realize it until I heard the bushes rattle. When I heard the bushes rattle I turned around and he had an AR-15 pointed right at my face, I mean right at my face. I went, "No!" like that [Jesse raised his hands in front of his face protectively] and he pulled the trigger. The bullet went off my right hand [the edge], you can still see the scars, and

tore off the whole top of this finger [left ring] and then
shavings went through my left pinkie.

I wasn't even aware of what happened. I've listened to
guys talk about it before, and they say they get shot and it
hurt really bad, and I don't know if I always believe 'em,
because when I got hit I didn't even know it. It happened so
fast, it was instant. I dropped the gun, and his gun went off.
I didn't know it at the time, but the same bullet hit the cab
of the truck, too. Bob turned around and shot that guy in
the ankles.

By this time the helicopter was directly overhead, and it
was an army helicopter. They started to come down, and
there were guys with a megaphone going, "What's going
on? What's going on?" I could hear them talking.

I didn't know I was hit, and I reached down and
grabbed my rifle and I pulled my rifle up and when I did I
felt the blood hitting my arm. I felt it and it was like, "Oh
my God!" I freaked, I panicked for a minute. I didn't panic
that bad because I felt no pain. By this time I started moving towards the front of the truck—and all this is happening very fast—and these guys that were in the woods ran
back into the woods. I don't know what happened to them.
The guys in the pickup truck just jumped in the truck.
They eventually got caught, I know they did. But they
didn't get charged with anything; there was nothing ever
said about it.

The guys in the helicopter had seen just about everything that was going on. The only problem was that the
truck was backed up under these trees, these pine trees, so
they didn't see anything of me until I actually walked out.
Then they started leaving and I told Bob what had happened. I said, "Bob, I got hit, I got hit," and he looks at me
and goes, "It ain't bad." He turned around and fired a few
shots into the woods. Those guys split. And the guys in the
truck hopped in their pickup truck and just disbanded.

Bob goes, "Come here, let me see it." He looked at it

and said, "The first thing we gotta do is stop the blood." He took off his shirt and ripped it in pieces and put a tourniquet on my arm. We had gallons of water that we'd brought with us to drink, and he was dumping it on my hand. I could see the bone. It was bleeding like crazy, it was nuts.

The thing about it is, I never felt it. I was very calm. Medically, as it turned out, this one [left ring finger] was the worst. It hit a main artery through the center and some nerves and stuff. Now I don't have any problem with it. I play guitar, I've been playing for 15 years. The only thing is sometimes I get pinky lock from that one.

He wrapped my hands and stopped the bleeding. He wrapped up both my hands, and one thing he said that made me feel a lot better—and I've seen a lot of his pictures and heard a lot of stories of the things he'd seen in Nam— and he told me that I reacted better than most of the guys he'd seen over there get shot. That gave me a lot of confidence. For a 15-year-old kid, I was scared shitless. He says, "Here, drink some of this," and I drank a whole bunch of vodka. I was getting toasted anyway, so I wasn't really too worried about it.

He went back to start the truck, and the truck still wouldn't start. We were kind of stuck there. Still had this baby, Judy was still in the truck lying down on the floorboard. She goes, "What's going on, what's going on?" She's yelling. He's like nothing ever happened: "It's all right, there's nobody out here." I couldn't believe this guy was acting so rational about this, but I guess he'd probably seen a lot of shit in his time.

He hopped on the bike and went for a ride and said, "I'll be back." We waited and we waited, long time went by. I had been drinking, and I ate some of this guacamole dip, Doritos and guacamole dip. I got sick as a dog. And during the time that he was gone I got really toasted.

Finally he came back. Well, there was a car coming,

and we could see the dust coming off the road. Just couldn't really see the car. I started to get really paranoid, so Judy and I thought it would be best if we walked back in the woods. We didn't know if it was those people again, we had no idea. Bob got out of the car. He wrecked the Triumph up the road and ended up walking out, and he found these people and they brought him back. We tried the truck again, the truck still wouldn't start. So these people took us to the ranger station.

We told the ranger that we had found the baby, and that this was a hunting accident. That's what we said, because there was a police report and I had to go into detail. I said that we were hunting rabbits and I shot and the bullet ricocheted off a rock, that's how we said it. There was a report made and that's all there was to it.

The helicopter followed that truck that was running through the back roads. At that point we didn't know what happened to that. They were caught because they were driving recklessly and the helicopter was chasing them . . . We gave [the rangers] the baby, said that we found the baby, they were like cool, they took the baby. They rushed me down to Cheyenne, to the medical center, and took care of these. They shot a bunch of novocaine, actually they gave me a couple shots first, then they shot a bunch of novocaine in. They had two doctors, or actually a doctor and a male nurse, working on each side. They were scrubbing the shit out of me. They just kind of bandaged me up and this sheriff came and asked what happened . . . We went back to the house and got Judy's car, got a bunch of tools so Bob could work on the truck, and we went out, put the key in the truck, and it fired right up. Too weird.

Jesse, now 26, is in college studying business administration.

K.C.

We were going to a convention, and I was driving three people in my Chevy Blazer with magazines and so on. Les was in the back, and he found an old knife that I'd forgotten about. A hunting knife. He said, "Hey, boss, what are you doing with this?" It had a compass on the end, you know. It's not a stick-em knife, it's a fish knife or whatever. He found it because we had pulled up the seat. It hadn't been used since who knows when. It wouldn't even come out of the sheath.

So all the way out there Les is taking this thing in and out, in and out, until it came easily out of the sheath. I wasn't thinking anything else about it. I dropped them off, stayed a couple hours.

I'm driving back into town, it's not even that late, it's only about one in the morning. I get out of the truck, and I'm wearing a three-quarter-length jacket with deep pockets on either side. Here's this knife lying on the seat that Les had found, and to this moment I can't tell you why, but I took the knife and put it in my left-hand pocket. I got out of the truck in the parking lot and started walking to the hotel, which is only a half a block. I had a gold chain on my neck, and it's a good one and it doesn't come off.

Next thing I know I've got a guy around me pulling the

chain. These are kids, and they got me from behind. They were amateurs or they fucked up. He's trying to get the chain off my neck, and the other guy came up around me and they left both my arms free. I'm left-handed. With my right hand I held onto the sheath through the jacket and with my left I pulled the knife out of my pocket. I pulled it out, thrust it out, and the guy just came right into it.

I had never stabbed anybody before. Now I'm trying to get it out, and with all the jagged edges [the sawtooth spine on the knife] I'm ripping the shit out of this guy. The other guy is still pulling on my neck, he doesn't care. In the meantime, out of the darkness on the other side of the street, I see five or six black dudes coming out—not to help me, but to help them.

Thank God a cop car is coming down the avenue. They see what's going on and they jump out. The five guys disappear back into the shadows they came from. The guy around my neck started to run, and they probably radioed someone else because they caught him running down the street, another police car did.

The policemen were great. I told them what happened. I was totally in control. And they found a vial of coke on the ground. The guy was bleeding to death, I'm telling you. An ambulance came and all that. This was right before the [Rodney King] L.A. riots. Had it been after that, forget it. None of what I'm telling you now would have happened, I'm sure.

I told them who I was, and I said, "I can't have any publicity behind this. I'll be guilty even if I'm innocent." One of the cops named Peters rode a Harley and I said—the only lie I told them—that I have a son that goes to a local university and there could be retribution.

I'm this big, burly, bearded biker that stabbed this one young black guy. They understood it fully and said, "Hey, we'll take care of everything, just go to your hotel." And I didn't hear anything since. I would have pressed charges, but they said all it would mean to them was serious paper-work on their part. What I'm guessing happened is they charged the one guy with attempting to rob the other guy and drug possession.

I knew the one cop's name, Peters, and I wanted to know, not how's the kid, but what happened. I called a few days later and he said, "Please don't call me. Everything is all right." Now the L.A. riots are happening. He said, "Don't talk. It's over. Forget about it." To this day I don't know if the guy's living, dead, I don't know what happened.

I went to Les and I said, "Les, if you think about it, you saved my life." He said, "Don't say that, boss, it's bad luck." In Hungary it's bad luck for me to say that. And I had to let Les go about a month and a half later.

I was fine. They gave me my weapon back. I was calm, I was cool. It was the next day I got the shakes like you wouldn't believe. Started trembling all over. Couldn't make the convention.

The main thing, when I saw those five people across the street, they were gonna take my shorts, everything. I saw it coming, like, "Hey, we got one." They were gonna kill me.

I'll never forget it, and I'm happy about how it came out. Looking back, it did feel good.

K.C. is the publisher of a motorcycle magazine. He travels a lot.

Mitch Trivitt

IT REGROUPS YOUR WHOLE THINKING PATTERN, MAKES you realize what everything's worth. Makes you appreciate stuff. Don't make me appreciate my friends too much because my friends is the ones that done it to me. Not all of 'em, but . . . you gotta watch 'em.

See, it was a friend of mine that done it to me, a friend for 10 years, a friend I'd never thought would have done nothing like that to me. That's who shot me. Because he was drunk. That's what alcohol will do to you. He was drinking for maybe six hours, down in Maryland.

I was in New Jersey visiting a friend, and I came home and he was sleeping in the car. I woke him up, told him to get out of the car and come on in the house because it's nice and cool in there. [He did get up and come inside.]

They were sitting in there talking about, they had this little kitten, they were gonna see who could fuck this kitten. Just stupid shit because you know they was drunk. I was just minding my own business. Him and the guy that I lived with, Jeff. Him and Jeff, they were really good friends, they grew up together, got along well. It just took this one time.

Me and Jeff, we spent about two hours one day putting a ceiling fan in the ceiling. Ceilings, they're kind of flimsy in a trailer. They were drinking like I say, and arguing over who's going to fuck this cat first—which was a good laugh, is what it was. Stynie stood up, the one who shot me, and put his hand in the ceiling fan and jarred it loose from the ceiling. After we spent all that time trying to put it up.

Jeff was standing there, and it pissed him off is what it done. He just turned around and slammed him, pushed him up against the wall, and he hit the wall and then he hit the floor all in the same movement. Jeff picked him up off the floor and threw him out of the trailer. Jeff is probably about 250 pounds, about six foot, I'd say. He went out the door and kept pushing Stynie up the hill. The way I look at it now that it's over, that probably agitated him pretty good, you know?

I was sitting there doing bong hits at my kitchen table and I looked up and Stynie was sitting up there on his porch. I turned around to do another bong hit, well, it just happened that quick. He shot, and you could hear it, I could feel it. Nobody else felt it, I don't guess, because nobody else got hit. But I couldn't get off the chair. It happened that fast. He shot nine times. Out of nine only eight went off and five hit me—three in my back and two in my arm. I couldn't get off the chair and I couldn't breathe. My lungs and everything collapsed, and he shot through my trachea tube and one lodged in my neck.

I went over to Jeff and I was kind of hugging onto him. Can't breathe, I couldn't talk! I was trying to yell but it was only like a whisper: I can't breathe, I can't breathe! And Jeff, not knowing any better, started beating me on the back and said, "If you don't breathe now you'll never breathe again." It was like I started to come out of it, you know, from him beating me on the back. I went outside the door and I leaned, put my hands on the fender of the car, and I was leaning there and trying to regroup and it felt like I was coming out of it. Now I'm gonna be all right.

Stynie thought that it was Jeff sitting there. Me and Jeff had the same color shirt on, and I was sitting in Jeff's chair, where Jeff always sat. He just had a habit of sitting there. And he must have thought that it was Jeff there, because he shot. I'm sure it wasn't meant for me. I was just a sucker.

Anyway, like I said I was lying on that fender and I thought I was coming out of it, then all of a sudden it was gone. It just left. I fell down on the hood of the car, like my arms just kind of gave out. I was gone. I was losing it. Dying is what I think was happening. You had your last inspiration and now it's time.

Jeff just came out and picked me up, he's a big guy, it wasn't nothing for him to pick me up, he just picked me up and set me in the car. His old lady was there, Sue, and he told her to take me to the hospital and don't stop for nothing and that's what she done.

I was freezing. It was June 19, '88. It was a hot day. She was flying down the street there and I'm freezing. I told her, "Put the windows up." Then a couple minutes later, "Put the windows down." It was cold, then it was hot, then cold. I was in shock, going in and out of shock.

When I got to the hospital I got out of the car, on my own, and walked through the first set of glass doors. I met some old lady, some old lady was pushing a wheelchair. She was coming out to get me. Well, I passed her, through the second set of doors. I just walked right by her to the emergency room and lay down on one of their tables back in there.

They already knew what was going on because somebody called. I just laid on the table and all I heard them say was, "He's going in, now he's out." Going into shock. They cut my clothes off of me, and I woke up three days later. Couldn't talk. Had this tube, big old tube, down my throat, tubes up my nose, tubes in my side, tubes everywhere. You could feel you was all swelled up, you just felt like your head looked like some kind of basketball or something. I wouldn't ever want to go through it again, and I don't wish it on nobody.

I was in 14 days, Hanover General Hospital. Nine days critical care and five days out in a regular room just to make sure I was all right. They kept me on morphine. They had to take me off the morphine because I was getting addicted, it was starting to blow my mind. I'd walk down the hall and all of a sudden I'd just start fading away.

The one [bullet] went in my side, my right side, and came out my stomach on the left side about four inches below my belly button. The other one went in my shoulder—they didn't have to take that one out, it never did come out. The other one went in the top of my shoulder; it went straight through my trachea tube in my throat and everything and lodged in my neck. They never did take it out because it's a 50-50 chance you might live and you might not, through the operations. Let's leave it there, and they told me a callus would build around it and I wouldn't have to worry about it. So far it's done pretty good.

I'm all numb, the whole back of my arm's numb, one side of my chest's all numb. The one that went down here [stomach] severed a nerve in my right leg, and I can't get around heat. Too much heat makes my leg go out. I'll get a real sharp pain then all of a sudden my leg'll go out on me. I lay blacktop. And I mean, it bothers me. It's sore, but you just gotta fight it, you can't let it get you. Let it hurt.

The guy that shot me, he turned himself in—it happened on a Sunday—he turns himself in on a Wednesday and said, "Oh, I heard I shot somebody. I just wanted to know if I did or not." What's that? Either you shot somebody or you didn't. He was smart enough, after he shot me, he wrapped the gun up in his daughter's clothes and slid the gun up underneath the couch, then took off running. It's not like he didn't know what he done. You're drunk, you're drunk. I ain't never been that drunk. You know if you do something like that.

I had a colostomy for four months. You shit in a bag. The one here blew my intestines apart. They cut 10 inches of intestinal tract out. You just gotta put up with the bag—which some people put up with for the rest of their lives. I was lucky, I was real lucky, mine was able to be sewed back together. It wasn't destroyed that bad. Most people who live with it forever, it's because of cancer or something like that.

It's a weird feeling, you know? I don't sit with my back to a door anymore. I like to face the door or at least be to the side of it. I don't sit with my back to the door anywhere. It's a habit.

Stynie had a bad habit. He liked to drink, but he wasn't known for fighting. What he was known for, see, he had a rifle—he had the .22 he shot me with and he had an Argentina rifle, I'm not really sure of the caliber. Maybe 30 days, a month before he shot me, he had pulled that gun on a Puerto Rican who was a good friend of ours. He pulled this Argentina out on this guy, Tommy, and shot over his head. Me and Jeff, we didn't think too much of it at the time, but we took the gun from him. Beat his ass, sent him home, destroyed the gun. I think we should have learned from that, the guy was capable of just about anything. But we didn't. We should have took the other gun. But you never know.

It's a person out of the blue that'll do it to you. Somebody you least expect will do it to you every time. I never in this world would have thought he'd have been like that, that he'd do something like that. Not to me, or even attempt to do it to Jeff. I mean, after all the years they growed up together. I was friends with him for 10 years. I was working for him at the time. We was building houses, setting modular homes. Him and Jeff, like I say, they went to kindergarten and everything together, and he still attempted to shoot him. You'd never have thought that. Just out of the blue. Somebody gets to drinking, gets on alcohol, and you can't judge their actions. They can change, *snap*.

133

As far as I know, Stynie had never been in a bar fight. He was a real quiet guy, kept to himself. He was just funny. I've had my friends say to me, even before he shot me, "What's wrong with that guy?" Because he's so quiet and he stares, you know, he don't talk. He's just quiet. They're the ones you gotta watch, the quiet ones.

There was a guy there, his name is Jeff Trish. I might have met the man once before I got shot. But the night after I went in he came to the hospital and he was at the hospital every night. I mean from the time he got off work to the time they throwed him out, which some nights they let him stay there till 10, 11 o'clock. He was there. And I never really knew this guy at all, but now today he's my best friend. A perfect stranger, he was there every day, more than I can say for my brothers or anything. My brothers, they don't like hospitals. They've been in and out of them so many times, and they don't care for them anyhow. But this guy took out of his time, out of his leisure time, out of his family time, he spent every night with me. There wasn't a night he didn't show up. That tickled me to death. Somebody that'd take the time out of their schedule to be with somebody like that, that they don't even know, is a hell of a man. I ain't got no bad words to say about that guy at all. He pulled me through. Him and one nurse.

They had this tube down my throat. In the evenings they'd have to strap my hands down to keep me from pulling this tube out of my throat. Strap me down to the bed. I couldn't move hardly anyhow but my arms a little bit to write or draw or something. If I wanted to talk to somebody I had to write everything down. The nurse, Janet Thomas, she'd get off around 9, 10 o'clock at night, at the hospital, she'd sit there with me till sometimes 2, 3 o'clock in the morning. Just to be with me, you know, just to spend time with me, knowing that I had an old lady—it's not like she was getting after me or nothing—she just wanted to make sure I was all right. I gotta thank her too. She's a helluva girl.

The people are the ones that pull you through, otherwise you'd have a tendency to give up. Why am I even fighting it? What's it all worth? I'm gonna go back out there and it'll happen again, and maybe next time I won't be so lucky.

[The guy that shot Mitch Trivitt went to prison.] Yeah, he did. Five to ten years. He's eligible for parole in '93. They fed me a cock-and-bull story where I could sign a paper and he'd do another five, but you know how that goes. The state's paying for him, and they're gonna let him out. If they let him out, they let him out. As long as he don't come around me it'll be all right. I ain't gonna go looking for him because that ain't gonna prove nothing.

The guy was a good friend of mine, that's where I stand. I know he didn't mean to shoot me. That's what makes it so hard. He was a good friend of mine, but he got ignorant. It cost me, and I just don't know where I stand as far as me and him, you know? I don't like losing a friendship, they're too hard to find. But there's gotta be a limit somewhere too. You don't gotta worry about me and him going out drinking, you can bet on that. I can blame the guy, but I can't hold it against him for the rest of his life. Alcohol does stupid shit to people. I mean, I've done some stupid shit on alcohol. I've been in jail already because of some of the stuff I've done. I just can't hold that against him. You drink so much you don't know what the fuck you're doing. Alcohol is another name for ignorance.

He was passed out in a car and I woke him up. Should I have let him sleep? Something good might have happened if I woke him up, you never know. Something other than being shot. You just don't know, you can't predict it. When it's gonna happen, it's gonna happen. There ain't a damn thing you can do about it.

I was shot in the back. That's the part that really rips

my ass about it. Why would somebody . . . if you can't face me face-to-face, don't bother with me. If you ain't man enough to stand in my face if you have a problem, you don't resort to violence like that, as far as shooting somebody. It ain't worth someone's life because you're mad. You gotta respect another person's life. You might not respect the person, but at least you don't end their life for them. I don't understand. I'm still confused about it.

Mitch Trivitt is a good man and a tremendous help when you're broken down on the road. Where he now lives, you couldn't get a shot into the front door.

James Mahaffey

A COLLAPSED LUNG IS VERY CLOSE TO CHILDBIRTH, IT really is. All the muscles in your body contract to take up the empty space. Your entire torso goes snap into a giant charley horse. It just makes you nuts.

This thing happened in Houston, Texas, in a place called Montrose. It's like right up against downtown. It's a real rundown area of the community, where all the hippies and the gay people live and so forth. It was 1975, February 12, when it happened. It was around 11:30 at night. My old lady and I had been out and had dinner and a couple of drinks. We were having a good time and came home and we were sitting in front of the tube watching Johnny Carson or whatever the hell it was, and the dog was there and everything was under control.

We were living in a relatively inexpensive apartment that opened out onto a courtyard with a swimming pool in the middle. You get into the complex through a lobby where the post boxes are. It's a room about 20-foot square, and you got a door coming in and a door that comes out into the patio and pool area.

It was quiet and we were having a glass of wine. Then all of a sudden it was like the whole building began to reverberate, like somebody dropped a bowling ball three times, real fast.

We both got up and the dog was going nuts, all over the apartment. I go to the door and I open it. And my best friend Kevin was standing there. I go out onto the patio and send the dog back inside, and Kevin's looking up at the second floor. I glance up and see this long-haired guy and two chicks, and they're stomping down the walkway that goes around the complex. And they're headed for the stairs that lead to the lobby. They're all 20 to 25.

Behind them is a door with three holes in it where the guy had hit it three times with his hand. Kevin looks up at the guy and says, "Hey, what's your problem, fellah?" One of the girls is carrying a half-filled hurricane glass. The guy's face turns inside out, he's so pissed off, and he screams, "None of your fucking business!" I'm looking at this guy and despite the fact that he's completely out of control, I'm empathizing with him because I know exactly how pissed off he is. I've been that pissed off myself.

From behind Kevin, the owner of the apartment [building] who lives in one of the other apartments down-stairs screams, "I own these apartments and it is my fuckin' business." The whole thing is like watching a movie. I can't remember seeing somebody so ripped up and twisted when he communicated. And the long-haired guy commu-nicated. And then Gladys [the owner] flipped in exactly the same way. And she's this nice little old lady from East Texas. I never heard her use that kind of language before.

The long-haired guy comes down from the stairwell and says, "Back inside and nobody'll get hurt." Well, that's the wrong thing to say to Gladys. And the assistant manag-er is upstairs, he's standing there in his underwear and he's got a .357 Magnum in his hand. Gladys says, "Al, go get his license number and I'll call the police."

I look at Kevin and I said, "Come on, let's go talk to these clowns." Me and Kevin were going to talk to this guy and mellow him out and get him to come back and explain to Gladys that he had a little too much to drink, that he'd replace the door, that it was not a problem. That's basically what our mission was, because Al was not dealing with it very well.

Kevin nods and we walk across the patio into the lobby. We're about 5 or 6 feet into the room and I see a silhouette of this long-haired guy framed in the doorway. And the reason I can only see a silhouette is that Gladys is so cheap that she never replaces the fuckin' light bulbs. This room is dark. There's no light except the light coming from the street and the light from the pool area. We go into the room and this guy's standing there in the doorway and his right hand comes up and he says, "I told you motherfuckers to stay inside." And I could see the knife.

"Kevin, he's got a knife" was all I could say before he was on us. He made his first stab at Kevin, because Kevin's bigger than I am, I guess. I moved around to my right, deeper into the lobby, to flank him. That was a big mistake because I moved into a corner I couldn't get out of. He's sort of concentrating on Kevin, and he follows around in this move with the knife and he cuts through my shirt. I got a new work shirt on, a new chambray work shirt. He cuts through the shirt and the tip of the blade just kind of scrapes across my stomach. I literally contracted my body away from the blade as he made the pass at me. All of this took place in like half a second.

In every crisis situation I've ever been in, all of a sudden everything stops. It moves in slow motion and I've got this sensation of being outside myself and watching this happen. So the guy makes a forehand move on me and he cuts my stomach, just barely. He made a backhand move and he cuts my right chest to the bone. And it wasn't until he actually cut me that I realized I was in a fight.

In my peripheral vision I see Kevin booking, he's heading out the door. Everything was kind of happening so fast and I didn't know whether he was running away out of good sense or he was running away because he was frightened. And at that point I didn't care.

So the guy makes a pass. He's made a forehand pass and a backhand pass. And then he makes a forehand pass across my face. I pull my face out of the way. He doesn't get me. Then he makes a backhand pass. When he makes the backhand pass, I used my right arm, I bring my right arm down to block the pass and with my left hand I go with my thumb into his Adam's apple. He goes down, the knife goes down, and we're scrambling on the floor for the knife. He comes up with the knife and I grab both his wrists with my hands and put my thumbs into the soft part inside. He's got the knife with two hands. We get it up and I can see there's only about three-quarters of an inch of blade left.

I just pushed him away from me, and by that time Kevin came back with four or five guys and they got him. I walked out into the pool area to find out what this guy's done to me. I've got this cut on my right chest and I'm bleeding like a stuck pig. I put my hand over that and walked back to the apartment. Inside the apartment, the dog has gone totally berserk, he's completely nuts, and my old lady's just standing there. I come through the door and she goes crazy. I said, "No, no, just mellow out and I'll go see how badly I'm hurt." So I go in the bathroom and I peel off the shirt and I've got this cut about four inches long, and it looks like butchered meat. I said, "Aw fuck, I've got to get stitches."

So I'm a little bit shocky. I come out of the bathroom with a towel on my chest and say, "It's not really serious, but I've still got to get a few stitches." And by this time the entire apartment complex is in my living room. Everybody makes me lie down. They've got an ambulance on the way. When Kevin comes back, I say, "You know this is crazy. There's no reason to take an ambulance. We'll get in the car and we'll go."

My old lady gets her purse and everything, and she gives the keys to Kevin and says she can't drive. We get somebody to watch the dog and we go to the emergency room, which is about 10 minutes away. Kevin's driving and he's stopping at the stoplights and everything, just for a minute, and then he'd drive through. By now it's midnight. He wants to get me to the hospital fast, and I'm going, "Slow down, guy, it's no big problem. It's just a scratch." We get about three minutes away from the hospital and my right lung collapses. Just folds up on me.

It was like somebody hit me in the lung with a baseball bat. *Bang*, that fast. I go forward in the seat and I go, "Oh shiiiit." And he says, "What's wrong?" I said, "Something else is wrong. I don't know what it is, but you better get me there fast." He just floors it, he's running red lights and all kinds of shit. We get to the hospital, and I remember walking into the emergency room with the towel on my chest and saying, "I've been stabbed," and they take me straight into the emergency room. I've got one arm around Kevin's shoulders, and they get me up on the gurney and they cut away the skin and I look down and I can see this blade sticking out of my chest. The left side of my chest.

The blade is sticking out and I can see it, about half an inch. Up until then I'd had a John Wayne complex. I'd been a good American, I'd lived up to my culture and done everything exactly the way it was supposed to be done in the movies, except I'd done it a quarter of a second too late.

He'd driven the blade into my fifth rib, so when I brought my arm down I broke the blade off. If it had been a good knife I'd have fucked myself up, but because it was a cheap knife I broke the blade off instead.

They got me on the table, and there was an hour of questions, and I'm trying to get all this shit out of the way so I can have some surgery. They're going to open up my diaphragm, and I know if they open up my diaphragm they're going to open me up and see if there was any damage to my liver or anything like that. They get my lung pumped up and I'm screaming at them, "I want some Librium and I want some Demerol."

They said, "Are you a drug addict or what?" Finally the registered nurse said, "These people are confused, you're prescribing drugs for yourself. What's the problem?"

I said, "I need the Librium to stop the contractions in my chest because the muscles in my body are trying to make up for the empty space where my lung used to be. And I need the Demerol to stop the pain." And he said, "Oh."

The surgery did more damage to me than the knife did.

At a time when he was on the lam from the feds, James Mahaffey was appearing regularly as a TV soap opera actor under another name. He is now teaching in China.

Mike

I WAS JUST OUT WANDERING AROUND. I'D HAD LIKE TWO beers and it was, "Well, let's go check out where the kids walk near the river." The L.A. River is a 45-degree embankment which is stones covered with Gunite, so it's real sharp, but they got a walkway beside it and I'm walking along.

White Oak is a real peaceful neighborhood, it's just close to Birmingham High. There were three people. One of them walked up to me straight, so I figured he was the leader of the group. I wear ivory and turquoise. He pointed to my ivory bracelet and said, "I want that."

I looked at the guy and I'm going, "What?" and he says, "I want that," and he kept walking toward me. When he was like 2 feet, right in my face, he crossed the line. You just walked too far, kid.

These were high school students. It was like 2:30, 3 o'clock, so they just got out. He kept walking toward me, not even looking at my hands, so I grabbed his ears and hair. The thickest part of your skull is your forehead, right above the flat part, and the thinnest is where the nose is, where the sinuses are. When people head-butt each other, you can go forehead to forehead, that's cool. It just shows you don't pass out easy. I don't do that. I go forehead to front of face, because it breaks a lot of real thin bones.

So the first kid walks up and says, "I want that ivory bracelet." The guy was like a foot from me, looking at me. And I thought, holy shit, he thinks he's run into a hippie, because I was wearing overalls with patches and long hair and such. The guy thinks he's run into somebody who's for peace and whatever. I look him square in the eyes, put my hands up, because they were relaxed by my side, which is a real good posture, grabbed him by the ears, and pulled him into my forehead. And the guy passed out.

His friends decided to throw me down the embankment, which is real sharp. I reached out with both hands and grabbed both of them, and we all three went down. I only had scratches on my legs, but I'm sure they got 'em all over. I hugged one guy real tight because I didn't want him on my chest. I don't need any more scars on my chest. I've already got six inches of scar on my chest, I don't need any more. That, and I've had enough broken ribs.

So the three of us go tumbling down to the flat bottom of the L.A. River, which is all concrete. The second guy, he seemed to be the taller of the bunch, pulled out a Rambo knife and held it at me. I said, "Okay, cool." He took a real low slash at me, halfway between knee and thigh. The first dig in was about an eighth to a sixteenth of an inch deep. The weird thing was, I looked at my overalls afterwards and there wasn't a scratch on them. He didn't cut the overall. He stuck me through the threads, and when he went up, I backed off.

My overalls have a nice little pocket on the right side low on the right hip. I loosened my knife, Old '71. It's a butcher knife, basically, with a handle as long as the knife blade, which is about 4 inches.

I didn't want to hurt him. I really don't want to hurt people. I really don't like it, it makes me nauseous. I especially don't like hurting greenhorns. If these people had been bikers, it would have been, "Okay, I'll ruin you real good." But they were kids, coming home from high school, that decided to do something to some dumb-ass hippie. So when the guy hit me in the thigh I stepped back, and as I did the knife pulled out of the cut. I grabbed my knife from the side of my overalls, came up with it, and ran it across one nipple and over the other nipple. I didn't want to hurt him, but I wanted to let him know, "hey guy, you've done something real bad and you oughta split."

The guy at the top, the first thing I'd said to him was, "You really don't want to do this to me. You probably want to do it to someone else, but you don't want to do it to me." And he said, "Oh, yeah, right man." Well, I broke his face. Where the guy clipped me with the knife, it's about a 2-inch cut, all healed now. This was about two months ago. I worried about him dipping it into shit. I used to do that with my knives. I heard the Vietcong did it with punji stakes, so it was like, if some son of a bitch is trying to kill me, I'll put something into him that'll rot. I don't care.

So I hit this kid from his right nipple across to his other nipple, right across the rib cage. I didn't want to cut into the rib cage, because that's real messy and you'll kill somebody. I didn't want to slash his throat. I wanted to teach him a lesson. So I hit him from left nipple across to the right shoulder, which left my knife about head high: *You wanna do something else, guy? Walk on into me.*

He sort of fell down. Most people, when they see their own blood, they pass out. I think it's a riot. I see my own blood and I think it's time to move. I'm not one of those who passes out at the sight of blood. But the kid was, and I wiped the knife off on him. The third guy kept on backing up and backing up and he took a run at me. I do something which is called a cat's paw, fingernails at the same level as the palm, and I hit him square in the chest with that. He reeled back. He looked at his friend, who was blooded from nipple to shoulder, and they decided that they were going to leave me alone.

They ran up to the top of the embankment, and the

guy there hadn't gotten up yet. They picked him up and walked off. I thought, holy shit, they're going for their friends. My thought was to get the hell over the fence and walk. I didn't want to meet their friends. Their friends could have guns. In fact, I think the guy that was the head of the group, the guy that I butted, had a gun. I talked to a friend later and I said, "Gee, I wonder what they're going to tell their parents?" He said, "They got attacked by a bunch of Mexicans." I thought that sounded about right, five or six Mexicans instead of one deranged hippie, slightly drunk and on a number of pills.

I don't care what I do to you. You fuck with me and you're going to learn a lesson. This guy had stuck me in the thigh, and he deserved to get cut. He cut me and I pulled out a real sharp knife and gave him something to remember me by. When he gets old, he'll go, "Yeah, this is a knife wound, man. Fourteen guys did this to me."

I had this wicker basket with me, about three feet tall. I walked up the hill at like a 45-degree angle and threw the basket over the fence and climbed over after it—ripped the back of my pants—and went home. I decided not to tell my wife, and she said, "Ah, you fell down the embankment, jeez, that was really stupid." I'm thinking, well, she really doesn't want to hear that I cut somebody. About Wednesday—this happened on a Monday—I finally said I'd actually been mugged and this is what happened. She said, "Jeez, I wish you'd told me. You don't seem so stupid when something like this happens."

I've got luck. I got shot, but the best possible scenario when you get shot happened. I've been mugged four times, and all four times I've said no for one reason or another. This time was the same thing, I just said no. You want to rob me? You don't realize, I've been studying yoga since I was 12, martial arts since about 15, and now I'm 38. I'm past the stage of, "there's 14 moves to take somebody out." I'm at the stage where there's only one way to do this. The kid at the bottom will need stitches; the kid at the top I think will need a few surgeries to make his face look good.

I really don't like fighting. When I was 17 to 25, I'd go into a bar and piss somebody's cigarette out to start a fight. But jeez, I'm old enough now that my wounds take twice as long to heal, and they hurt even worse.

Mike lives as full and interesting a life as he can. He resides in the San Fernando Valley area of Los Angeles.

Joanie Argento

THE GUY THAT I WAS GOING OUT WITH, WHO DID IT, WE had broken up. We had a bad relationship for like five years on and off, on and off. The last time we broke up I went out with someone else for like 10 months, but I got in a fight with the guy and I hit him with a bottle and we broke up. Then I went back to my first boyfriend.

We went to a HOG [Harley Owner's Group] party, and we were hanging out, drinking, and we had a great time. Then we went back to the bar where we hung out. He was drinking Jack, of course, the devil's brew, and someone took the bottle because he was getting too drunk and acting ridiculous. When they took the bottle he got more mad than he had been in the first place—started a big fight, took out the gun. "I want my bottle or I'm gonna fuckin shoot all of youse." The whole shit. So they gave him his bottle back.

Eventually it led to an argument. He knew I was sitting there going, "You're an asshole," started a big fight and I started crying. My girlfriend came over to see if I was alright and he started cursing her out. At that point I said, "Leave her alone, she's got nothing to do with it. I want to leave."

Okay. We got in the car outside the bar, and sitting in

the car he started pushing me, hair pulling, the whole bit, and I was thinking, "When I wake up tomorrow morning, that's it, this is over with." And I guess he knew it. He said, "What's the matter, you afraid? You won't hit me back the way you hit Richie back. You won't hit me with a bottle or I'll kick your ass." And he said, "Here, you want to even the odds? You scared, you want to even the odds?" He took the gun out, click, and put it on my leg. And when he put it on my leg, *boom*, it went off.

I felt it, but I didn't feel pain. I felt it hit me but then I wasn't in immediate pain, so maybe I didn't get shot. I felt my leg. I had white pants on, I felt my leg and pulled my hand up and there was blood all over. I said, "You fuckin' asshole, you shot me." That's exactly what I said.

He just left me in the car, ran out of the car screaming like a crazy person into the bar, "I shot her!" Everybody was stoned out of their minds, it was like 4 o'clock in the morning. Next thing I know there's like 20 people outside and I'm sitting there with my leg hanging out of the car, like, "What are we gonna do?"

This guy, Carl, who's a good friend of ours, pushed me in the car, pushed him in the car, shut the door, and started driving to the hospital. On the way, my boyfriend's screaming bloody murder and I'm sitting there saying, "Just drive. Wherever you're taking me, just drive." We got there and of course the whole 20 people followed us. And the outside door was locked.

He wanted to tell the cops that he did it. I didn't want to tell them, because it was an accident. Whatever kind of reasoning that was, I have no idea. We finally got in the hospital, and it was totally ridiculous, running through the hallways with the stretcher like I was dropping dead, and I said, "Hey, take it easy, guys, I'm only bleeding from my leg."

We get inside and me and Carl, the guy who drove us, try to get a story together. We just decided to say there was a fight, whatever, and the guys ran. Then they left me alone and they wouldn't let anyone else in the room. That was the only point I was scared, when they left me alone with the doctors and the staff. They wouldn't let any of my friends in. One of the girls said she was my sister. Nothing. They came in and said, "All right, we have to give you a tetanus shot," and that was the only point that I cried. Oh no, a needle.

They just let me lie there for awhile. They cut my pants off, and they had a specialist come down. The doctor said he didn't know how close it was to a vein or an artery or whatever. The doctor came down and said he didn't think it hit an artery. The first doctor came back and said, "We think it came out, but we have to take an X-ray. If there is a problem, there can be a point in time where they have to cut your leg off." And then I was like a crazy person. Because before I was just like, "I got shot in the leg, no problem, who cares?"

They took me in for X-rays and the cops came and started asking me all kinds of questions. I was scared shit. The cop said, "You couldn't have gotten shot from that far away because there are powder burns, very bad, on your leg." I said, "I don't know how far away the guy was." And it was a bad move because the angle was downward on my thigh so it looked like I did it myself. But we stuck to the story and there was nothing they could do.

They took the X-ray, said it was fine. They cleaned me up, no stitches, no nothing. They kept me there for five or six hours, shots, needles, blood, the whole shit. Then they said I could go home. Someone came to pick me up and I went home.

I was fine for a day. Then after that day I sat down and started thinking, like *holy shit*. I have a son, and he was a baby at the time, just about a year. We went home and [the guy who shot me] was totally incoherent, for like two days you couldn't talk to him, nothing. I took it as a joke. My boyfriend wrecked the house, said, "It's not funny." Somebody came over and found the shell and gave it to me.

I went back to the doctor to get checked. He said, "Do you realize that you could have been in for a month if it would have hit an artery or a vein? We would have had to make skin grafts. If it would have hit a bone you would have been in here four months, maybe six months. About another two inches and you would have been dead, because there's an artery that goes straight to your heart." I was like, "Get the hell outta here!" I had *no* idea. From that point on I was like schizo, because they told me I could have died. And that's actually when the pain started, because I tore a piece of the muscle. I couldn't sit or bend, it would rip, and I'd have to clean it and I'd cry, thinking crazy shit.

We broke up like a month after that. I actually went back with him twice after that, too. Some sick shit. And like now, the other day it was very cold and rainy—every time it hurts I hate him. At the gym, with the left leg, 40, 50 pounds no problem. With the right leg, 20 pounds. It took me almost a year to get them even. But it still hurts. It's a crazy thing. The doctor told me it won't ever go away totally. The winter it gets cold, numb. It stays colder than the other leg.

Psychologically, it fucks you up. We went out four months ago, and the guy who shot me was there. I still see him, we're still friends. He still walks around with the gun like it never happened. Stupidity. He was playing around and he took it out, and I thought I was going to faint. I said, "You're a jerk, how could you play around like that?" He took it out later and put it in front of me to show me, and I started screaming and crying. I feel like now if somebody tried to mug me or something and put a gun to my face, I would either drop dead or rip the person's eyes out. It's a scary thing. I don't want to get shot again.

No one hangs out at that bar anymore; we all hang

out at another bar. The other night I left about 3:30, I said to my girlfriend, "I've had enough of this shit. Everybody's drunk, they're retarded." We left and they called me the next day. One of the guys had shot out the mirror behind the bar. If I had been there I would have died. It's a scary thing.

To me now, I can joke about it. But seriously, when there are fights in the bar—I'm still always around bikers, you can't change what you are—when there are fights and I'm around, I'm always outside because of that fear that somebody's going to pull a gun and start shooting.

As for what happened to me, I joke about it. That's how I deal with it.

Joanie works for a major airline in one of America's busy airports.

Vic Noto

I GUESS IT WAS A COUPLE YEARS AGO IN THE SPRINGTIME. I was headed down to the gym in downtown Manhattan. I got off one train and I was running down the stairs, I was going to grab another train.

This fuckin' lowlife was sitting at the bottom of the stairs. There were people in front of me, and somehow I banged into the guy a little bit, said, "Excuse me," and ran to catch the fuckin' train. The Q train. The doors closed and I missed it. Now I'm on the platform with this guy and he starts shooting his mouth off. I don't know what race this guy was. He was a weird-looking motherfucker, he looked like he had 15 different races in him. Like he was the United Nations or some shit.

So this fucking guy starts rattling some shit off to me like, "Can't you watch where you're going?" and this and that. I said, "Look, let's get something straight right now." I'm there in my T-shirt, and I got 18-inch arms. I'm a little guy, I'm 5 foot 7. This fucking guy's about 6 foot 1. I said "Excuse me. I didn't do it on fucking purpose, you know." I tell him I'm not the average kind of white person yuppie guy with a tie and a briefcase. "You know what I mean? I'll smack the shit out of you. You're dealing with the wrong white guy." I'm not a regular white person that takes shit from people.

So this fucking guy stands up. It's springtime, like 70 degrees, and this guy has a long coat, like a Civil War coat down to his ankles. And he's pulling something out of his fucking pocket. Now me, being the law-abiding person I am—you know what the law says you're supposed to do? The law says that you're supposed to wait for the guy to take the weapon out and cut your throat or shoot you in the fucking spine, then they want you to crawl to the phone and call 911. I'm supposed to wait for this motherfucker to take whatever it is out of his pocket and use it on me, so then I can kick his ass. That's what the law is telling me and everybody else we're supposed to do, right?

So I told this motherfucker, "Pull the fucking thing out of your pocket. I don't give a shit what it is, pull it out and let's go." So he pulls it out. I don't know what it is yet, because he's got it hidden in his sleeve, like he's got one fucking arm, right? And he's waving this thing, I don't know what the fuck it is. But I went to kick it out of his hand and just missed. He takes the fucking thing out and throws it at me, and I threw my right arm up to fuckin' block it and it cut me on the arm. *Bang*, it hit the fucking deck.

It was a 12-inch railroad spike. It came from the subway tracks. He must have pulled it out. A rusty railroad spike. So now he's running, he's running away. Goes up the stairs, going along the platform. I picked the fucking thing up, and while I'm running I put it in my bag for evidence and all that other shit later. Which became a fucking joke anyway, and you'll find out why.

This was a time where I'm working out at the gym, but I'm still smoking like three packs of cigarettes a day. I've since quit, but I'm fucking huffing and puffing and this motherfucker's running full speed. There's these three homeboys down there and they said, "Yo, you want him?"

I said, "Yeah, grab the motherfucker." So they grabbed him. And I'm huffing and puffing.

There was some guy that was right up there where the homeboys were, and he's some kind of transit worker. Obviously he either saw what happened or he knew what was going on, and he starts on the walkie-talkie calling somebody.

I was pissed off. I grabbed this fucking guy, put him in a headlock, and started banging his head against the fucking wall, right? There was a poster there and I kept banging his head. He's bleeding and every other fucking thing, and I look up at the poster, and it was a subway poster for the movie *Lethal Weapon 2*. It was funny as hell. The black guys are cracking up, slapping five: "Yo, man, look at the fucking poster!"

Now the guy breaks away from me and he runs away. He runs downstairs and there are all these cops all over the place. Must be 50 fucking cops there. This motherfucker talks to this high-ranking cop, he's got scrambled eggs on his hat, he's a lieutenant or something. So this cop comes up to me, and the guy with the walkie-talkie told him what happened, and I told him this fucking guy threw this thing at me that I had in my hand.

They had caught the fucking guy, but the lieutenant comes over there and winks to me and goes, "You didn't hit him, did you?" I said, "No, not me, sir." Played it like this Eddie Haskell routine. Apparently this guy told them that I kicked the shit out of him, banged his head against the wall a million times.

So they arrested the guy. About two weeks later—I had given the cop my phone number, address, the whole fucking thing, you know—the district attorney calls me on the phone. This broad. We're talking and talking, she wants me to sign this fucking paper and this and that. I said, "I would be very curious, do I have the right to know what this guy's rap sheet is?" She says, "Absolutely. I'll get it for you and

I'll call you back tomorrow." And she called me back the next day. Basically, I did society a favor, because this motherfucker had a rap sheet a mile long. He had attempted-murder bench warrants on him for not showing up for court, fugitive warrants all over the fucking place. The guy was a sick motherfucker, he was a punk.

The wrap-up on this whole fucking thing is this: I'm waiting for some kind of court date or something. About two weeks later I get this message on my fucking machine that's like two days old because I wasn't home for two fucking days, saying I got to get into the district attorney's office tomorrow to sign the fucking paper and if I don't they're gonna cut this guy loose for some reason until he's gotta go to court.

So these motherfuckers fucked up, they cut the guy loose. They called the district attorney's office back and said, "He's gone and he's never going to come back." So he's out in society carrying railroad spikes in his fucking pocket.

Vic Noto is a film actor. At this writing, his most recent work was 29th Street *with Danny Aiello. When not working, he rides his Harley-Davidson Super Glide.*

Big Daddy

WE WERE IN RICHIE'S ONE NIGHT, THE WHOLE CLUB was there. Three guys walked in wiped out of their minds on Quaaludes. Quaalude monsters. So they started in with Wild Bill. Wild Bill told the kid, "Hey man, just get out of my face, alright, cause you're gonna get hurt. I'm telling you and your friends, just get out. We're tired of you, we're not bullshitting."

The guy left and came back about an hour later. Now he's even more wasted than he was before. We're standing around, and he pushes Bill off the stool. Bill picks this piece of steel out of his pocket, from somewhere he got it, found it in the street or something, this piece of leaf spring. *Whisssht,* rips the guy right open. Oh, Jesus, here we go.

So I grabbed a guy. I told the guy three times he should leave. Little glasses-wearing faggot motherfucker. I told him, "You gotta leave, man, because you're gonna get seriously hurt." He says, "I can't leave, they're my friends." One of those attitudes. "Alright, but I'm telling you, when the shit kicks off I'm gonna put you right in the beer cooler."

Richie's was a rectangular bar. When the shit kicked off, he was the first guy I grabbed, *whoosh, boom,* right through the beer glass into the cooler. Beer went all over the place, the manager was pissed. It continued outside for about 20 minutes. One guy went to the hospital for eight months. They're still looking for his balls. A circle formed on him you know, and he wouldn't go down. He was so whacked out of his mind on Quaaludes he couldn't feel anything. Even when his head got slammed in the car door he couldn't feel it. He was still talking, jabberjabberjabber. Unbelievable shit.

We were down to the Mavericks' clubhouse one night, we were partying. We steady partied with those people. We were like the overlords of Hudson County. We had come to power in 5 years. We took great pride in having that kind of power, but we also didn't push our weight around unless it was necessary. So we were at the Maverick's clubhouse and we were partying. The party persisted, it got a little out of hand. I was standing outside with one of the Mavericks, drinking. And he recognized these two guys. They had come up the night before and ripped up the clubhouse.

I had never seen Yente go off. Yente was my brother. He was a Maverick but he was *my* brother. I consider him my brother. I'd never seen the man go off, know what I mean? He's got a full pitcher of beer in his hand. *Bang*, he smacks this guy right in the forehead. I said, "Holy shit, what's up, man?" I went to grab his buddy and his buddy took off. He takes off, runs into his van and locks the door.

Yente chases his partner down the fuckin' road, caught him over by the Hideaway, caught him right up in there somewhere in the parking lot, and finished him off. Yente comes back, and I'm by the van trying to talk to this kid and telling him he's gotta leave.

"What?"

"Listen, man, you gotta get the fuck outta here. Nobody wants you."

"What?"

We did that for about 20 minutes and now I'm pissed. I'm not having a good time, my brother Yente is upset, my other brothers are upset. I said, "Why don't you open this door, man, so we can talk" (laughs). So he was stupid enough to open the fucking door. I grabbed him. *Bang.* "Gimme all your fuckin' money, cause I don't hit nobody for free."

He says, "I don't have a job!"

I said, "Get a fuckin job!" *Boom*, and I smacked him again. So I come back and the president of my club's walking up the fucking street, and I'm grumbling, "That motherfucker's got no goddamn money I punched him in the goddamn face for nothing scumbag motherfucker started a fight couldn't believe it motherfucker got no bread no job he's a fuckin loser . . ." And I'm going past everybody, they wanna know what I'm grumbling about. So I told Yente, I said, "His partner's leaving now, as soon as he wakes up." He says, "Oh good. If he don't wake up soon we'll drive him out of here."

Chops was an Alien prospect at one time and never made the grade. Unfortunately for me and my brothers he tied up with us and rode with us for a little while. He still never made the grade and turned out to be a real shithead again.

He came up one night and claimed that my brother Jack had taken his Sportster and wasn't giving it back and he owed him money for storage. I said, "Well, listen, man, sure, we'll take care of your problem. We'll get your sled back, cause I ain't into taking nobody's sled. We'll get your sled back and everything'll be cool." So he ran his mouth at my president's house. Why my president didn't just shoot him I have no idea, because the guy just got obnoxious. I mean, I have a tolerance for people, but a guy comes in my home and runs shit on me, whew, World War II immediately commences. That shows disrespect, and I don't go for that ever.

So I went down by the bar and Jack's there, and this guy's there, and we're talking. I said, "Jack, do me a favor and give this guy back his bike." Alright. We got everything all settled. He's gonna get his bike back and everybody's happy. The Chops says, "Well, I put a contract on him."

I said, "Well that's no problem. Get on the phone and drop a dime and cancel the contract. That's fair. I mean, I'm getting your bike back for you. I'm not going to let you kill one of my brothers. I don't care what happens, but if he goes down, you're going with him. Simple as that."

Now he's drunk and stupid and he's in my face. I said, "You know, man, I've had enough of you." *Boom.* He had false teeth and I took the first one right out. He was down. And I proceeded to beat him into the fucking ground because I hated him at that point. So I look down and I have his tooth sticking out of my knuckle. I hope he doesn't have rabies.

I walk in shaking my head and bleeding. I'm not so much mad that I'm bleeding and I have his tooth, I was mad at the fact that things could have come out easier without all this bullshit. People get that Budweiser in them and they can't do nothing. Beer muscles. It was all settled, and he got his bike back after he recovered. He was almost dead when he left where I was. I kicked him right in the fucking throat. I had my boot heel on his Adam's apple. He was gonna die. He got me to the point where I just didn't see him anymore, all I saw was the end result, Alligator Alley out in the Meadowlands somewhere, you know.★ Jesus Christ, he's nothing to me. My brothers are my brothers.

The Skyway Riders approached us one time down at Richie's about some stolen motorcycles. This guy comes up, Clown. Clown, Bozo, whatever. And he brought his big-mouthed old lady with him. She was kind of cute actu-

★ *The Meadowlands is an enormous swamp area in northern New Jersey that has served as a dumping ground for many bodies. Giant Stadium is in the Meadowlands, and Jimmy Hoffa is said to be under that great football shrine.*

ally. My brothers wanted to do things to her, but we didn't want to start an international incident since they were only a block away and there were 40 or 50 of us in the bar.

We told them, "First of all, we wouldn't steal your bikes since you all ride Jap bikes. You ain't nothing but a bunch of fuckin' squids to start with, and we don't need Jap bike parts, so there'd be no reason for us to take your fucking motorcycles. Second, we just don't do that shit. Everybody here's got titles for their sleds, and if not then the club has the title because we loaned them the money for it."

Well, she starts, "Who the fuck do you think you are babeepbabopbaboop." I says, "Clownie, you know, your old lady has more balls than you do, man. That's a goddamn shame. Woman comes here with you and you can't keep your old lady quiet for 15 whole minutes. That's a fucking shame, to be a punk."

He says, "I'm no punk, she just has a mind of her own." I said, "Well, my old lady don't run her mouth. I tell her to go home, she goes home. I tell my old lady to shut up, she shuts up. How come your old lady don't know those words? What's the matter, you do the dishes at your house?"

Now he figures that he's a little fucked up. About 20 of my brothers emptied out of the bar and we have a little powwow on the corner: "Look, man, we told you, we ain't got your fucking bikes. Don't come up here no more. It's our fucking bar and we don't want you here. And if any of your fucking boys down the road there think they're tough enough to come up here, send 'em up and we'll send 'em back." They were directly around the corner. And they stayed there too.

I can tell you a funny tale, and it's true. I had two partners at one time, we had a business in South Hackensack. And my partners were worthless, absolutely worthless, 100 percent. They had patents on being nothing, that's how much nothing they were. They had this guy Walter who used to hang out with us. Walter wanted in the worst way to be impressive to somebody—anybody! He didn't care who you were, just anybody. You could be 85 years old, and if he impressed you he was happy. So the guy, his nickname was Fly, he was in the bar with his old lady, and Walter and his old lady and I walked in the bar. We'd all been living together in the same apartment, and Walter owed my old lady—not this one, my ex-old lady—money for babysitting. About 80 dollars, and things were tight, business was slow. So we went around and around in the bar. We come out, and I'm in Walter's face, and Fly gets real stupid and gives Walter one of his two sheath knives. I said, "Walter, are you really going to use that knife on me?" He says, "If I have to."

That's all I wanted to know. I punched him a shot in the jaw and dropped him like a bad habit. He laid there right in the street and didn't even move. He wasn't moving, and I wasn't even sure he was breathing. I punched him dead in his face. So his old lady's there: "I'm sick of this shit!"

I said, "Me too. Every time I punch him in the face he don't get up so I can finish the fucking job. What kinda fuckin' wimpy old man did you fucking marry?" So I walk up the street. Somebody pisses on Walter or something and wakes him up, and he comes running up the street. Now Fly's handed him a .25-caliber semiautomatic pistol. He's winging the knife back and forth and I got a couple good shots in, kicked him in the thigh a couple times, smacked him a couple times, then *pow!* and I heard *bzzzzzzz*. I know that sound, I've heard that before. I said, "Well, you motherfucker, you took a shot at me. You scumbag. I'm gonna fucking kill you, man." All of a sudden the lady of the house hears the commotion, and there's cops, and they drag us in.

We're in Hackensack Police Department. We're sitting in the same fucking like area, and I said to Fly, "You better get out of Jersey, man. I'm gonna hunt you down until you're too old to walk, and then I'm gonna shoot you right in the fucking head. Better get out of Jersey. You violated the fucking laws of the streets, man. My fucking streets."

Round and around and around and around. Finally the next day we were released on drunk and disorderly. They found no gun. They confiscated Fly's knives, which were totally illegal, and he posted some kind of bullshit bail. Couple weeks later we go to court, and I grab Walter on the side. I said, "Look, Walter, it's not that I don't like you, it's that you're an asshole. When we're in front of this judge, do something fucking smart for once in your life. You got a drunk and disorderly charge. It's a $50 fine. Plead guilty to it, tell him it'll never happen again, and he might let you walk. You get fucking stupid in front of that judge, and this judge is gonna put you in jail."

We go up in front of the judge together and he calls out our names. I said, "Look, your honor, me and Mr. R——have made up and we're apologetic to the court. We're really sorry for the disturbance and it'll never happen again. We were wrong and we're sorry." Judge says, "All right, $25, $10 court costs, get out of here. And don't come back." At that point in time, Fly stands up and pleads not guilty to possession of the knives and not guilty to inciting the fight. When we left he was still pleading his case. I think he did a year.

There was one time in Hoboken . . . Hoboken was funny. We were hanging out there many, many years ago, even before the Hoboken MC was started. There was another club in the area, and we knew members of the club. And we were hanging out, talking to some pretty little señoritas down there. These two guys came in and shoved one of my brothers. Naturally, words were exchanged: "You motherfucking spic cocksucker, cut it out."

"I'll go upstairs and get my chotgun and choot you!"

He runs upstairs and we run upstairs after him. We

don't know what this fucking guy's got. One of my brothers was extremely large. He was 7 foot 2 inches tall and he weighed 505 pounds. He made the center patch look like a postage stamp. We get upstairs, we duke it out with the Puerto Ricans, we take away their shotgun, and we were preparing to throw them out the second-story window. We figure they didn't have far to go. They won't die, they'll just get bruised.

The cops come.

My one brother's got this guy by the collar of his shirt and the seat of his pants, and he's swinging him out the window. Cop says: "Put that guy down!"

"What'd you say, man? Put him down?" Right underneath the window was a cast-iron radiator. "You want me to put him down right here?"

"That's right, put him down."

"Now, put him down?"

I don't know if you've ever been picked up by a 7 foot 2 inch man, but his waist is about four feet off the ground, and when he picks you up with his arms curled, you're up about six feet. He says, "Okay, I'll put him down!" _Clang._

"Wise fuckin' ass. Get downstairs." So we get downstairs. He tells my one brother, "Get your hands on the wall and don't move. And you, you big motherfucker, you put your hands on the second story and if you even sneeze I'm shooting you, because I don't have anything that'll hold you down."

So my brother turns: "You funny bunny little punk ass cop, I've beaten up bigger dogs than you."

There were a lot better times. Violence is something. You revel in it when it's over, but you don't revel in it at the moment. When it's over and you find that, well, in my case the club I rode with was very large, and when you turn and look around and you see maybe one black eye, that's it, that's the better part of the whole deal. Squids shouldn't cross into where they don't belong.

Like now, I'm a lot older, and I'm on parole, for violence. You have to go into a situation with a different outlook. Jail doesn't scare me. It wasn't that bad. They lock you up, you're confined and you're alone. Before I got married the second time I was alone for 10 years, so it's not a problem. I was on my way to doing a lot of good things before, and they take everything. You come out with nothing.

As you get older, you want to see the young guys do it, if anything. Let the 21-, 22-year-olds do it right. Maybe there's hope for the cycle world after all, maybe there are people out there that are really solid. And maybe there's not. Today, daddy loans you $6,000 to buy a Harley Davidson. Well I bought mine for $70 a week until I paid off the $1,200 dollars I owed the guy that owned it. Now people out there got tattoos and long hair don't even own motorcycles. And it seems like they're content to be that way, even though I know, and they know, that they're from a different life-style, era. And the violence doesn't reign there.

A lifelong biker, Big Daddy was once shot by a robber who took 72 cents from him. That story is in Lead Poisoning.

Danny Machuca

IT WAS MAYBE 3 O'CLOCK, 4 O'CLOCK IN THE MORNING, and I just came out of a wedding. A friend of mine had gotten married, and I was kind of drinking.

His wife, his new wife, tells me, why don't you go walk my girlfriend to the train station. I'm a little bit tipsy, and I'm like, I really don't want to go. She says this and that, and after a while she convinced me. This was at Myrtle and Wyckoff, in Brooklyn. It was me, my friend, and two girls walking to the train station. It's kind of late and the neighborhood is kind of bad.

We dropped them off, and me and my friend are conversating, I forget what we were talking about. All of a sudden four guys are coming up the block that we were going down. My friend looks over to me and asks me, "Do you know any of them?" I said "No, why?" He said, "Because they're looking at you." I guess they thought I was familiar or something.

I turned around and they were all turning around, you know? Plus I was wearing all this jewelry on me, not thinking it was probably the jewelry. I had a nice bracelet, I had a nice chain.

Then they said something and we started walking toward them. He must have said something like, "You fucking prick," something like that. As we're walking toward them they started walking away from us. They just kept walking toward where the buses are. And we said, "Excuse me, what you say?" It was like, fuck you, this and that. It got into a shouting match. And we're a little tipsy, we're feeling okay, then all of a sudden one said, "Shut the fuck up and take off your chain."

Out of nowhere he pulls this little gun. I said, like, get the fuck out of here. He said, "You don't believe me?" My friend was a couple feet away from me on my right, and my back was against a steel gate. Three of them were in the street and he was right in front of me on the curb, where the sidewalk finishes. He was right there and his friends were behind him, and me and him were having this shouting match going on. He takes out his gun from his coat and starts pointing it at me. I'm thinking, aw, he's not going to shoot. But he just started shooting.

He wasn't catching me. He was shooting at the gate. He wanted the chain, so he shot maybe four times at the gate. I heard things ricocheting, and my friend said, "Danny, Danny, just give it to him." All this was happening, and then he just stopped shooting. His gun just went *click*. It must have jammed, and he started running.

Me, being the ass that I am, I figured the gun got jammed and I'm going to chase him. His friends are running, he's running, I'm running behind him, my friend is running in back of me, and we had this wild chase. The chase was maybe two blocks, and all the time he's running he's playing with something.

All of a sudden he just turns around and he stops me right dead in my tracks. Just turns around and shoots me. You know, I'm running and then all of a sudden I feel something. *Boom.*

I was like, oh, man—I couldn't believe it. This couldn't happen to me. My friend catches up to me and I said, "Take me to the hospital, take me to the hospital." I see myself, and I have blood all over my chest. He's going crazy, he couldn't believe it either.

There's no phones around there, so we started walking. Seven blocks. Seven blocks until an ambulance passed. My friend waved it down. They had patients in the ambulance, and they told the patients, "Get off, get off!" I don't know what they had, I guess they weren't that sick, but they told them to get off. They started giving me life-support systems, and they rushed me off to Elmhurst Hospital.

The bullet collapsed my lung and went straight down. They couldn't get it. The doctor told me if it had been a bigger caliber or been over 2 inches it would have hit my heart. I guess I really was lucky this time. I still have the bullet in my stomach muscles.

All from trying to be brave. Sometimes the situation passes before my eyes and I try to analyze it and wonder how I could be so stupid. I was in the hospital for two weeks, then I was out of work, out of school, for like six months. I was 18.

It leaves a scar on you mentally. You can never really forget about the situation. You go back to it in your head. When I left that party, I didn't want to go. You know, sometimes you get that feeling like, don't go, don't go. Stay. I was getting that.

I don't understand how people can actually have guns and use them and not feel themselves that that could happen to them. It's a crazy world. You don't know how many people have given me advice. It was God, change your life, like that. I used to hang out with the guys, you know, not actually partaking in muggings, but seeing them. I used to stand on the corner and watch these guys truly victimize people. They're liable to stick anybody up. You don't have to be Spanish or black or white—they take anybody they can victimize without too much of a struggle. Everybody talks about racism and this and that, but it's not that way.

I can't begin to tell you the experiences I've had. I've

seen people cut open, I've seen people shot. But when it happens to you . . . It really made me think, "Wow, I got to change my direction."

Danny Machuca lives in New York City. At 21, he is studying with an eye to becoming an attorney.

About the Author

CHRIS PFOUTS' FIRST BOOK ON MODERN VIOLENCE, *Lead Poisoning: 25 True Stories from the Wrong End of a Gun,* was published by Paladin Press in 1991. Over a 10-year writing career, Pfouts has won several awards for his work. His reportage on violence, social history, music, motorcycle history, and tattooing has appeared in a number of American and European publications, and he enjoys a measure of notoriety as a music and literature critic. Pfouts resides in the United States and is currently editor of *International Tattoo Art* magazine.